Software Reliability Prediction Using Hybrid Jaya Optimization and Machine Learning Models

Solanki

TABLE OF CONTENTS

CHAPTER:1 Introduction

Software is a collection of data, instructions or programs that enable computers to perform specific tasks, serving as the interface between users and hardware. It encompasses various types, including system software (e.g., operating systems), development software (e.g., compilers) and application software (e.g., word processors). The success of software hinges on its attributes, which define its behavior, functionality, usability, and performance. These attributes are broadly categorized into functional and non-functional types, each playing a vital role in influencing the creation, implementation, evaluation, and maintenance of software systems.

Functional Attributes focus on ensuring that software performs its intended tasks accurately and comprehensively. Attributes such as correctness and completeness ensure that the software meets its specifications, includes all required features, and interacts effectively with other systems through interoperability. Additionally, traceability enables tracking requirements and changes, facilitating effective project management.

Non-functional Attributes, in contrast, address the software's quality and operational characteristics. Key attributes include:

- **Reliability**, ensuring consistent performance without failure.
- **Efficiency**, promoting optimal utilization of resources.
- **Usability**, emphasizing ease of learning and operation for end users.
- **Maintainability**, simplifying updates and modifications.
- **Scalability**, supporting increased workloads as demands grow.
- **Portability**, enabling adaptation to diverse environments.
- **Security**, protecting against unauthorized access and breaches.
- **Testability**, enhancing the ease of verifying functionality.
- **Flexibility**, allowing the software to adapt to evolving requirements.
- **Reusability**, facilitating the use of components across projects.
- **Extensibility**, enabling the integration of new features.
- **Availability**, ensuring system readiness for use.
- **Performance**, measuring speed and responsiveness.

- **Adaptability**, supporting adjustments to new platforms.
- **Resilience**, ensuring recovery from failures.
- **Configurability**, allowing customization without code changes.

These attributes collectively serve as benchmarks for software quality, guiding its creation to ensure it is reliable, efficient, user-centric, and adaptable to changing needs. By integrating these characteristics, software becomes not only functional but also robust and future-ready, establishing a strong foundation for addressing the evolving demands of users and industries.

Software reliability is a cornerstone of modern computing systems, ensuring that software consistently performs as intended and meets user expectations over time. In an era where software powers critical functions across diverse fields such as communication, transportation, healthcare, and finance, reliability has become indispensable. The impact of unreliable software can be severe, ranging from financial losses caused by system downtime to breaches compromising user data integrity. As software systems grow increasingly complex and technology continues to advance rapidly, achieving and maintaining reliability has become more challenging and more essential than ever.

It refers to the likelihood that a software system will perform its intended functions correctly without failure. This probability is measured over a specified period and under predetermined operating conditions. This concept encompasses several key attributes, including availability, correctness, fault tolerance, and maintainability. Ensuring high software reliability requires a comprehensive approach involving rigorous testing, continuous monitoring, and proactive risk mitigation strategies. Fault tolerance mechanisms, including redundancy and error detection or correction, are employed to mitigate the impact of failures and ensure that software continues to operate even when faults occur. Reliability engineering techniques, including failure analysis, fault prediction, and reliability modeling, are critical for identifying and addressing potential failure points throughout the software development lifecycle.

Thorough testing and validation are crucial for evaluating and improving software reliability. Employing testing approaches such as unit, integration, system, and acceptance testing is essential to verify that the software fulfills its requirements and performs as intended. Additionally, continuous monitoring of software performance and usage metrics enables the real-time identification of potential reliability issues, allowing organizations to take timely corrective actions. Proactive maintenance activities, such as applying updates, patches, and bug fixes, further address vulnerabilities and improve the overall reliability of software systems.

In today's connected world, reliable software is key to keeping critical systems dependable, secure, and performing well. By reducing downtime and protecting user data, it builds trust and supports smooth operations. Creating software that's strong and dependable not only meets user needs but also helps avoid costly failures or disruptions. By following solid engineering practices, thorough testing, and proactive maintenance, organizations can develop software that stays reliable over time. This allows them to keep up with users' changing needs and the fast pace of technological advancements, showing just how important software reliability is in today's digital world.

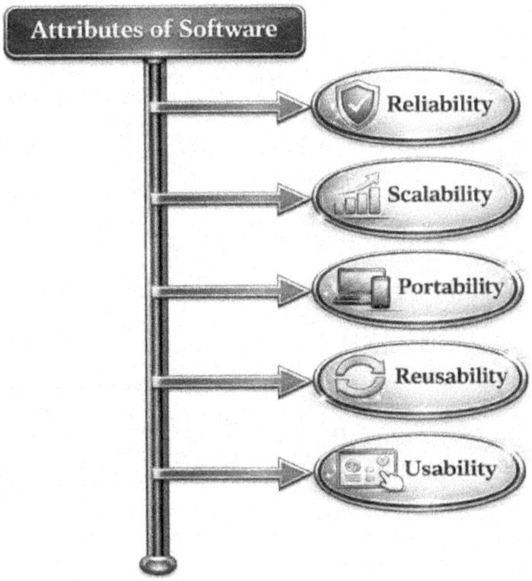

Fig. 1.1 Attributes of software

SRP is a proactive analytical process aimed at estimating the probability of a software system operating failure-free over a specified period under defined environmental and operational conditions. Unlike post-deployment reliability assessment, SRP is introduced early in the software development lifecycle to support informed design and testing decisions. The need for SRP arises from the increasing complexity of modern software systems, where failures can lead to significant financial loss, safety risks, and reduced user trust. By forecasting reliability metrics such as failure rate, mean time between failures (MTBF) and availability using historical failure data and reliability growth models, SRP enables developers to anticipate potential reliability bottlenecks and take corrective actions before system deployment.

Software Defect Prediction (SDP), although closely related, serves a fundamentally different purpose. SDP focuses on identifying defect-prone components or modules within a software system by analyzing code-level attributes such as complexity metrics, change history, and past defect data. ML and statistical techniques are commonly employed to classify software components as defective or non-defective. For example, in a large-scale enterprise application, SDP may identify specific classes or files that are more likely to contain bugs, allowing testers to prioritize inspection and debugging efforts. In contrast, SRP operates at the system level; for instance, in a safety-critical system such as an air traffic control application, SRP estimates whether the overall system can meet required reliability thresholds over continuous operation, regardless of the exact location of individual defects. Thus, SRP and SDP are distinct yet closely related concepts that can be clearly differentiated at the system level. SRP addresses the question, "How reliable will the entire software system be over time under given operational conditions?", whereas SDP focuses on "Which specific software components or modules are more likely to contain defects?" SRP provides a holistic assessment of overall system dependability and operational stability by estimating reliability metrics such as failure rate, availability, and failure intensity. In contrast, SDP offers localized, code-level insights by identifying defect-prone areas to support targeted testing and maintenance. Although SDP indirectly contributes to improving software reliability by reducing defect density, it does not explicitly quantify system-level reliability measures, which remain the primary focus of SRP.

In this thesis, SRP constitutes a core research contribution, where ML based and hybrid predictive models are proposed to enhance the accuracy of software reliability estimation. While SDP is discussed to establish conceptual context and to highlight complementary quality assurance techniques, the primary emphasis remains on system-level reliability forecasting. The thesis demonstrates how advanced learning models can outperform traditional reliability prediction approaches by capturing nonlinear failure patterns and temporal dependencies in software failure data. Consequently, SRP is not only introduced as a necessary concept but is also positioned as a central component of the thesis contribution, with SDP serving as a supportive and contextual framework within the broader domain of software quality assurance.

1.1 Objective of Thesis

The need for SRP arises from the increasing complexity, scale, and dynamic nature of modern software systems, where conventional reliability modeling approaches often fail to provide timely and accurate predictions. Traditional Software Reliability Models (SRM) are largely based on predefined statistical assumptions and failure rate distributions, which limit their applicability in environments characterized by evolving requirements, heterogeneous datasets, and nonlinear software behavior. In contrast, SRP focuses on learning reliability patterns directly from historical data, software metrics, and execution records, enabling proactive estimation of reliability during early and intermediate stages of software development.

To address this need, the primary objective of this thesis is to explore and propose innovative ML based methodologies for enhancing SRP. The research aims to overcome the limitations of conventional prediction methods by leveraging advanced algorithms capable of analyzing large and diverse datasets, including historical performance records, system logs, and other relevant indicators. The study systematically examines existing ML algorithms used for SRP, evaluating their strengths, limitations, and suitability across different application scenarios. In addition, significant emphasis is placed on data collection, feature engineering, and preprocessing to extract meaningful attributes that improve model effectiveness. While SRM primarily relies on parametric or non-parametric statistical formulations to model failure behavior over time, SRP adopts a data driven learning paradigm that emphasizes prediction accuracy, adaptability, and scalability. This differentiation is explained at a system level and supported by illustrative examples. The thesis further clarifies that establishing this distinction forms part of the conceptual foundation of the research, while the main contribution lies in the development, optimization, and empirical validation of ML based and hybrid SRP frameworks.

The thesis also focuses on developing and validating predictive models through experimentation with multiple learning algorithms, hyperparameter tuning, and the use of appropriate evaluation metrics. A comparative analysis is conducted to assess the performance of ML based SRP models against traditional reliability techniques in terms of robustness, accuracy, and scalability. In addition, the practical applicability of the proposed models is demonstrated through real world case studies, illustrating how SRP can be integrated into the software development lifecycle to identify and mitigate reliability issues at an early stage.

Finally, the thesis provides practical guidelines for researchers and practitioners on applying and optimizing ML techniques for SRP, and outlines potential directions for future research. By addressing the need for SRP and clearly distinguishing it from SRM, this work contributes to advancing the understanding and application of data driven reliability prediction, there by supporting the development of more reliable and dependable software systems.

1.2 Overview of Software Reliability

Software reliability is a crucial aspect of software quality, reflecting the likelihood that a system will operate without failure over a defined period and under specific conditions. It involves various measures and methods to ensure the software functions correctly and efficiently, meeting both functional and non-functional requirements. This overview will explore the definition, significance, factors affecting software reliability, measurement techniques, and strategies to improve reliability.

1.2.1 Definition and Significance

As a core element of software quality, software reliability denotes the probability that a program will perform its intended tasks successfully without failure over a specified period and under defined operating conditions. It is typically assessed in conjunction with other key quality indicators, such as a system's maintainability, functionality, usability, and performance. The significance of software reliability lies in its direct impact on user satisfaction, safety, and financial considerations. Unreliable software can cause catastrophic failures, especially in critical systems like medical devices, aviation, automotive systems, and financial services. Even in non-critical applications, software failures can lead to significant financial losses, harm to reputation, and decreased user satisfaction.

1.2.2 Factors Affecting Software Reliability

Several factors influence software reliability [1], including software complexity, the development process, team expertise, the operational environment, and maintenance and updates. More complex software has more potential failure points due to the intricacy of algorithms, interactions among components, and the sheer volume of code, all of which can introduce reliability issues. The methodologies and practices used during the software development life cycle (SDLC) significantly influence reliability; structured and well-defined processes, rigorous testing, and quality assurance practices typically produce more reliable software. The skills and experience of the development team are crucial, as teams with deep domain knowledge and proficiency in best coding practices are better positioned to create reliable software. The conditions, under which software operates, including hardware, network conditions, and user interactions, affect its reliability, and the software must be robust enough to handle variations in these conditions gracefully. Finally, regular maintenance and timely updates are essential to address emerging bugs and vulnerabilities, ensuring ongoing reliability.

1.2.3 Measuring Software Reliability

Reliability metrics are essential quantitative measures [2] used to evaluate a software system's dependability and robustness, ensuring that a system performs its intended functions without failure under specified conditions is essential. Key time-based metrics include Mean Time between Failures (MTBF), which calculates the average operational time between consecutive failures, and Mean Time to Failure (MTTF), which measures the time until the first failure occurs. Mean Time to Repair (MTTR) evaluates the average time required to restore the system after a failure, while the Failure Rate reflects how often failures occur during operation. Reliability, representing the probability of failure-free operation over a defined period, and Availability, indicating the proportion of time a system remains operational, are critical indicators of overall system performance. Further important measures include Defect Density, which evaluates the number of defects per unit size of the software, and Failure Probability, which offers insights into the risk of failure. Additionally, factors like Fault tolerance, Customer-reported incidents, Recovery time, and Service interruptions help measure how effectively the software handles faults, minimizes downtime, and maintains user satisfaction. Together, these metrics serve as benchmarks for assessing and improving software reliability, enabling organizations to build systems that are dependable, efficient, and user-centric. The failure rate measures how often software failures occur over a given period, with a lower rate indicating greater reliability. Fault Density quantifies the number of faults per unit size of the software, such as faults per thousand lines of code, where lower densities suggest higher reliability. An Operational Profile tests software under conditions that closely resemble real-world usage, providing more accurate reliability measurements. Lastly, Reliability growth models, including the Musa-Okumoto and Jelinski-Moranda models, predict improvements in reliability over time as faults are identified and corrected during testing.

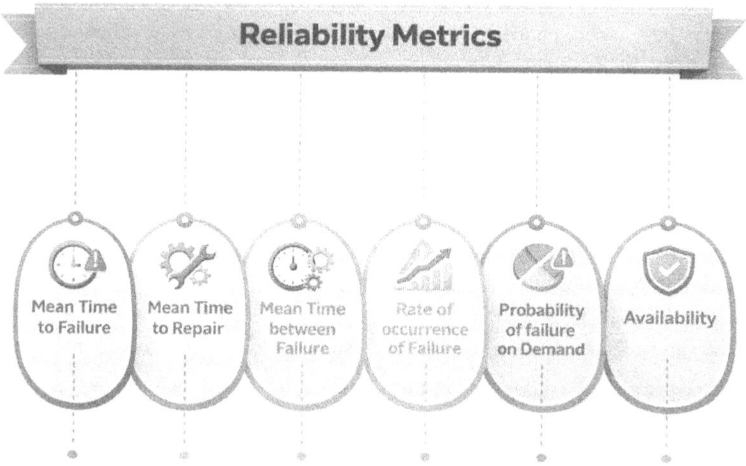

Fig. 1.2 Components of measuring software reliability

1.2.4 Strategies to Improve Software Reliability

Enhancing software reliability requires a comprehensive approach throughout the Software development lifecycle (SDLC), employing key strategies such as robust design and architecture, thorough testing, static and dynamic analysis, code reviews and inspections, error handling and recovery, continuous integration and continuous deployment, user feedback and monitoring, and regular maintenance and updates [3]. Ensuring a solid foundation through careful design choices like modular design, redundancy, and failover mechanisms can mitigate potential reliability issues. Rigorous testing, including unit, integration, system, and acceptance tests, is crucial, with automated tools and practices like Test-Driven development and Behavior-Driven development and Integrating testing into the development process. Static analysis tools detect potential issues without code execution, while dynamic analysis monitors software during execution to identify problems. Peer reviews and formal inspections catch defects early and promote adherence to coding standards. Robust error handling and recovery mechanisms enable software to recover gracefully from unexpected conditions, minimizing failure impacts. CI/CD practices help detect and resolve defects early in the development process by automatically testing and deploying code changes. This proactive approach is fundamental to upholding and maintaining software reliability throughout the product lifecycle. Post-deployment monitoring and user feedback help identify real-world issues not caught during testing, providing invaluable information for continuous improvement. Regular updates to fix bugs, patch vulnerabilities, and enhance functionality are essential for maintaining long-term software reliability.

1.2.5 Challenges in Ensuring Software Reliability

Despite best efforts, several challenges persist in ensuring software reliability, including changing requirements, resource constraints, technological advancements, and human factors. Evolving user requirements can introduce new complexities and potential points of failure, while time, budget, and resource limitations often force trade-offs between reliability and other project constraints. Rapid technological advancements can outpace the ability of development teams to adapt, leading to reliability issues. Additionally, errors and omissions by developers, testers, and users can all significantly impact software reliability.

1.2.6 Types of Software Reliability

Software reliability is segmented into different types based on factors like the software's nature, its usage patterns, and the specific reliability aspects under examination. One such category is Operational reliability, which specifically refers to the software's ability to successfully perform its intended functions during active use without failures, thus prioritizing real-world performance and error-free execution.

- **Structural Reliability:** Structural software reliability encompasses the systematic evaluation of software components' architectural, design, and coding structures to predict and enhance the system's capacity to operate dependably across different conditions [4]. It involves analyzing the relationships between modules, classes, and functions, identifying fault-prone areas, and quantitatively assessing reliability through metrics like cyclomatic complexity and code coverage. This analysis enables predictive modeling of software failures and defects, guiding improvement strategies such as refactoring, test coverage enhancement, and dependency mitigation. Integrated into the development process, structural software reliability ensures early identification and remediation of structural weaknesses, thereby improving overall quality and dependability of software systems.

- **Functional Reliability:** Functional software reliability pertains to the assurance of consistent and accurate performance of software functionalities under normal operating conditions. It focuses on guaranteeing that the software fulfills specified functional requirements and provides the intended outcomes without errors or deviations [5]. This involves rigorous testing of individual functions, modules, and the integrated system to verify their correctness, completeness, and robustness. Functional software reliability assessment encompasses various testing techniques to validate functional behavior across various layers of the software architecture. By confirming that the software functions as intended across diverse scenarios and user interactions, functional software reliability ensures a dependable and satisfactory user experience, contributing to overall software quality and customer satisfaction.
- **Performance Reliability:** A crucial aspect of software quality, performance reliability assesses a system's ability to consistently meet performance expectations under varying workloads [6]. The main objective is to ensure that the software functions efficiently in terms of response time, throughput, resource utilization, and scalability, which have a direct impact on user experience and system performance. Software engineers achieve this by applying evaluation methods such as load testing, stress testing, and performance profiling, allowing them to optimize performance and identify and resolve potential issues early in the development process.
- **Safety Reliability:** Safety software reliability refers to the ability of a software system to operate dependably while safeguarding users, equipment, and the surrounding environment. It involves the software's capability to perform essential functions accurately and consistently, preventing failures or errors that might cause hazardous conditions or accidents. This aspect of reliability is especially critical in fields such as automotive systems, aviation, healthcare, and nuclear power, where even minor software malfunctions can lead to serious consequences [7]. Techniques for

assessing safety software reliability include fault tolerance mechanisms, rigorous testing, formal verification, and compliance with safety standards and regulations such as ISO 26262 in automotive or DO-178C in aviation. By prioritizing safety considerations throughout the software development lifecycle, engineers can mitigate risks and enhance the reliability of safety-critical software systems.

- **Usability Reliability:** Usability software reliability pertains to the consistency and effectiveness of software in meeting user needs and expectations while maintaining stability and dependability. It encompasses the software's ability to provide a user-friendly interface, intuitive navigation, and efficient workflows, thereby facilitating a positive user experience. Usability and software reliability are crucial for ensuring user satisfaction, productivity, and adoption of the software [8]. Techniques for assessing usability reliability include user testing, heuristic evaluations, and usability metrics analysis. By prioritizing usability considerations throughout the software development lifecycle, engineers can enhance the overall reliability and quality of the software.
- **Scalability Reliability:** A system exhibits Scalability software reliability when it successfully accommodates increasing workloads and user demands without any drop in performance, responsiveness, or stability [9]. Achieving this requires engineers to design architectures and infrastructure capable of efficiently scaling up or down in response to changes in data volume or usage patterns. Because robust scalability is vital for handling growth without compromising reliability, it is assessed using methods such as load testing, capacity planning, and performance profiling. Integrating these considerations ensures the software remains reliable and fully operational even under varying conditions.

1.3 Software Reliability Models

Software quality improvement is inherently linked to software reliability models, as these models provide a structured approach to evaluate, predict, and enhance the reliability of software systems, which is a crucial aspect of overall quality. Reliability models focus on analyzing and quantifying how well a software system performs without failure under specified conditions, providing metrics and insights that directly contribute to improving software quality. SRMs are essential tools in software engineering, providing a structured framework to analyze, predict, and improve the reliability of software systems. They include various components, each playing a vital role in evaluating software quality and identifying potential risks and guiding decision-making throughout the SDLC [10]. With the goal of comprehensively exploring these components, their significance, methodologies, and real-world applications will be examined. Software reliability is defined as the probability that a software system will perform its intended functions without failure under specified conditions over a given period, underscores the critical importance of reliability in meeting user expectations, regulatory standards, and business objectives. As software pervades modern society, reliability models become essential mathematical and statistical frameworks, providing insights into failure mechanisms, predicting future occurrences, and facilitating decisions to enhance software quality and reliability.

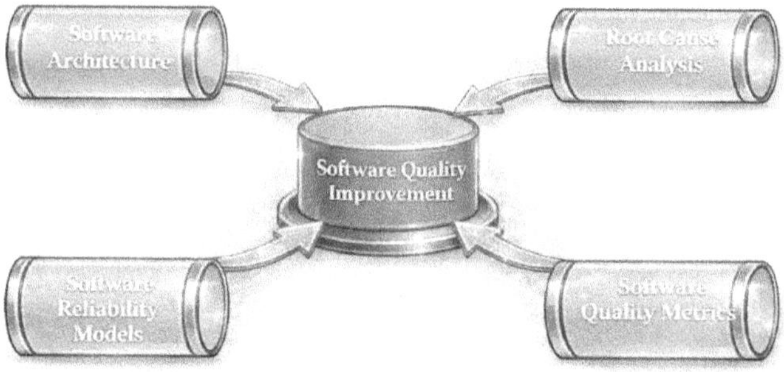

Fig. 1.3 Components of software quality improvement

1.3.1 Components Software Reliability Models

- **Failure Data:** Failure data is the cornerstone of software reliability modeling, comprising observations of software failures recorded over time, typically during testing, operation, or maintenance phases. This data includes details such as the timing, nature, severity, and conditions of failures, serving several critical purposes. It is used for model calibration by adjusting parameters to fit observed failure patterns accurately and for model validation by comparing predictions with actual data to ensure accuracy and real-world effectiveness. Additionally, failure data helps assess the current reliability of software systems, identifying areas for improvement and potential risks. Collecting and analyzing this data necessitates careful attention to quality, completeness, and relevance, with effective logging mechanisms, error reporting systems, and incident tracking tools being essential to ensure the reliability and accuracy of the data used in software reliability modeling.

- **Parameters and Distributions:** Parametric reliability models use specific statistical distributions to accurately represent software failure behavior, assuming that failures follow a particular probability distribution defined by parameters such as shape, scale, and rate. Common distributions used in these models include the Weibull, exponential, and log-normal distributions. Parameters for these distributions are estimated from failure data or historical information, enabling software engineers to effectively quantify and analyze software reliability. In contrast, non-parametric reliability models do not assume any specific probability distribution. Instead, they use empirical or historical data directly to estimate reliability, offering greater flexibility and adaptability to diverse data sources. These models are especially useful when the underlying failure distribution is unknown or when parametric assumptions are not applicable.

- **Time-to-Failure Analysis:** Time-to-failure analysis is a fundamental technique in software reliability modeling that focuses on understanding the intervals between software failures. This analysis provides critical understanding the reliability traits of software systems, revealing underlying failure patterns and trends that inform predictive modeling and decision-making. Two main techniques in time-to-failure analysis are survival analysis and reliability growth modeling. Survival analysis studies the probability distribution of the time until an event, such as a software failure, occurs, while accounting for censored data where failures have not yet happened by the end of the observation period. This approach helps estimate survival and hazard functions, providing insights into failure probabilities over time. Reliability growth modeling, on the other hand, predicts improvements in software reliability as defects are detected and fixed during testing and maintenance. It estimates parameters like initial failure intensity, defect discovery rate, and defect removal rate, enabling organizations to track and manage reliability growth effectively. Overall, time-to-failure analysis aids software engineers in assessing system reliability, identifying potential failure modes, and prioritizing improvement efforts to enhance software reliability and quality throughout the development lifecycle.

- **Software Metrics:** Software metrics are crucial for evaluating the reliability of software systems by providing quantitative measures of various aspects of software quality, complexity, and performance. These metrics offer valuable insights into the characteristics of the software code, aiding in reliability analysis, risk assessment, and decision-making processes. Common software metrics used in reliability analysis include code complexity metrics, code coverage metrics, fault density metrics, and change metrics. To identify error-prone sections of software that may need extra testing or refactoring to enhance reliability, code complexity metrics are used. These include Cyclomatic complexity, Halstead complexity measures, and McCabe's complexity metrics, which quantify the overall complexity of the software code. Code coverage metrics, including path coverage, statement coverage, and branch coverage assess the proportion of code executed during testing, providing insights into the thoroughness and effectiveness of testing efforts and their impact on software reliability. fault density metrics measure the density of defects or faults in the software code per unit size or functionality, highlighting areas that are more prone to errors and may need more attention during testing and maintenance phases. Change metrics, such as code modifications and change frequency, measure how often and how extensively the software code is altered, providing insights into the software's stability and reliability over time.

1.4 Types of Software Reliability Model

There are several types of software reliability models, each with its own assumptions, methodologies, and applications:

- Parametric software reliability model
- Nonparametric software reliability model
- Hybrid software reliability model

1.4.1 Parametric Software Reliability Model

Parametric SRMs are mathematical or statistical models used to predict, analyze, and improve how reliable software systems are. These models rely on specific probability distributions to represent software failure behavior accurately, assuming that failure occurrences follow particular distributions characterized by parameters defining the distribution's shape, scale, and rate. By estimating these parameters from failure data, parametric models provide a structured approach to understanding and improving software reliability. In this discussion, we will explore the categories of parametric software reliability models, provide examples, and support our discussion with appropriate references. Exponential distribution [11] models assume that software failures occur randomly and independently at a constant average rate over time. These models are characterized by a single parameter, the failure rate μ, which represents the average number of failures per unit of time. One important thing about the exponential distribution is that it does not remember past events, meaning the chance of a failure happening next is the same regardless of how long it has been since the last one.

This straightforward nature makes exponential models highly suitable for early-stage reliability assessments, where the failure rate remains fairly constant. For instance, the Jelinski-Moranda model [12] assumes a fixed number of initial faults and a decreasing failure rate as these faults are detected and corrected. Similarly, the Littlewood-Verrall model extends the basic exponential approach by adding parameters that better fit observed failure data. These models are often applied when the failure rate shows little variation over time, such as in the early testing stages of development, and they help estimate key reliability measures like MTBF. Similarly, Weibull distribution [13] models allow for varying failure rates over time, making them versatile for modeling software failure behavior in different contexts. These models are characterized by two parameters: the shape parameter β and the scale parameter η. The shape parameter β determines the failure rate pattern over time: for $<1\beta<1$, the failure rate decreases over time; for $=1\beta=1$, the failure rate is constant (similar to the exponential distribution); and for $>1\beta>1$, the failure rate increases over time. For example, the Weibull model is widely used in reliability growth models to represent different stages of software testing and operational use. During the debugging phase, β may be less than 1 as the failure rate decreases with bug fixes, while during the later stages of the software lifecycle; β may be greater than 1 if wear-out effects are considered. Weibull models are used in diverse applications, from initial software testing to long-term operational phases, allowing for a more detailed and flexible analysis of reliability over time.

Another parametric model, like log-normal distribution [14], captures the skewed distribution of failure times observed in many software systems by assuming that the logarithms of the times between failures are normally distributed. These models are characterized by two parameters i.e the standard deviation (σ) and the mean (μ) of the logarithms of failure times. For example, log-normal models are often used when failure data shows a skewed pattern, indicating that some failures are more likely to occur much later than others. This can be particularly useful in analyzing software systems with varied failure causes and effects. These models are useful in reliability engineering for systems where failure times do not follow a simple pattern but instead show significant variability. They are employed to estimate metrics such as MTTF and mean residual life (MRL). Gamma distribution models [15] are versatile for modeling software failure behavior with varying failure rates over time. These models are characterized by two parameters: the scale parameter θ and the shape parameter k. The gamma distribution is flexible and can capture both increasing and decreasing failure rates depending on its parameters. It is commonly used when the failure rate rises at first, as new faults appear or are discovered, and then falls as these faults are corrected.

During the initial deployment phase of a new software system, failure rates might increase due to unforeseen issues and then decrease as patches and updates are applied. Gamma models are applied in reliability growth modeling, where they can accurately reflect the complex nature of software failure processes over time. They are particularly useful in operational environments with varying workloads and stress conditions. Another most popular model Generalized Erlang distribution [16] models extend the Erlang distribution, allowing for more flexibility in modeling software failure behavior. These models are characterized by multiple parameters, including the shape parameter k and the scale parameter λ. The generalized Erlang distribution can model a wide range of failure behaviors by adjusting these parameters. For example, generalized Erlang models are used in systems with complex failure processes involving multiple stages. In a multi-phase software deployment where different stages (development, testing, and operational) exhibit distinct failure patterns, these models provide a more accurate representation of overall reliability. These models are applied in comprehensive reliability analysis of large-scale software systems with multiple interacting components and phases, helping to accurately estimate system reliability and identify potential reliability bottlenecks.

1.4.2 Non-Parametric Software Reliability Model

Non-parametric SRMs offer a flexible way to evaluate and predict software reliability without assuming any specific statistical distribution for failure times. Unlike parametric models, which are constrained by predetermined probability distributions characterized by parameters, non-parametric models are data-driven and can adapt to the actual observed failure data. This characteristic makes them particularly useful in scenarios where the failure behavior of the software is complex or unknown. We explore several categories of non-parametric software reliability models, each offering unique strengths and applications. The Kaplan-Meier estimator [17], also known as the product-limit estimator, is a valuable non-parametric tool for analyzing reliability. Its primary use is estimating the survival function by leveraging the observed times at which failures occurred. It is particularly effective in handling censored data, where some software failures are not observed within the study period. For example, in a software testing project, the Kaplan-Meier estimator can be used to estimate the likelihood that software modules will function without failure over time, providing insights into the system's reliability.

This model is widely used in survival analysis in medical research and has been adapted for software reliability analysis, particularly during the testing phase when data may be incomplete. Similarly The Nelson-Aalen estimator [18] is another non-parametric method that estimates the cumulative hazard function, reflecting the total risk of failure over time. It is especially effective for handling censored data and is often used alongside the Kaplan-Meier estimator. For instance, in a software development project, the Nelson-Aalen estimator can track the cumulative number of software failures over time, highlight periods of higher risk, and support proactive measures to improve reliability. This estimator is valuable in reliability engineering and survival analysis, providing a complementary perspective to the Kaplan-Meier estimator, especially in operational environments where understanding the cumulative risk of failure is crucial. Another model named Bayesian non-parametric models [19], leverages Bayesian statistical methods to model software reliability without assuming a specific parametric form for the failure distribution.

These models incorporate prior knowledge and continuously update reliability estimates as new failure data becomes available. For instance, in agile software development environments where new features and updates are frequently deployed, Bayesian non-parametric approaches integrate prior reliability knowledge and update estimates with new data, providing real-time reliability assessments. These models are highly flexible and adaptable to various software reliability scenarios, especially in dynamic environments, since the software's failure behavior can change over time, using such models is important. In a similar statistical context, kernel density estimation (KDE) is a non-parametric method used to estimate the probability density function of a variable. It is particularly useful in software reliability for deriving the failure time distribution from observed data. By applying KDE to observed failure times, researchers can obtain a smooth representation of the failure distribution, identify periods with a higher likelihood of failure, and guide efforts to improve reliability. Commonly used in data analysis and pattern recognition, KDE helps visualize failure patterns and reveal trends that may not be obvious from raw data, making it especially valuable for analyzing complex failure behaviors. The empirical cumulative distribution function (ECDF) [20] is a non-parametric estimator of the cumulative distribution function that, like other models, is built using observed failure data. It delivers a simple and intuitive means of summarizing failure information and assessing the dependability of software systems.

In a software testing project, the ECDF can be used to visualize the cumulative proportion of failures over time, aiding in identifying critical periods and evaluating the effectiveness of testing efforts. Fundamental in reliability analysis and statistical inference, the ECDF is especially useful for exploratory data analysis and when used alongside other non-parametric methods. Similarly, Bootstrap methods [21] involve resampling the observed failure data to generate multiple simulated datasets, which are then used to estimate the distribution of reliability metrics such as the MTF and the failure rate. In a software reliability study, applying bootstrap methods to observed failure data can generate confidence intervals for estimated reliability metrics, providing a robust assessment and accounting for variability. Bootstrap methods are widely used in statistical inference and are particularly valuable in software reliability analysis, especially when failure data is limited or highly variable. Another important approach is proportional hazards models [22], such as the Cox proportional hazards model. These semi-parametric models do not assume a specific baseline hazard function but instead assess the effect of covariates on the hazard rate, offering a flexible way to analyze software reliability. For example, in a software project, a Cox proportional hazards model can analyze the impact of different factors on the failure rate, aiding in identifying key drivers of software reliability. Widely used in survival analysis and reliability engineering, these models provide a powerful tool for understanding the factors influencing software reliability, particularly useful in multivariate analysis. Another model, i.e., graphical models known as non-parametric Bayesian networks represent the probabilistic relationships among variables. Non-parametric models are especially valuable for analyzing complex dependencies in software systems because they do not require assuming a specific parametric form for the underlying distributions. For example, in a large-scale software system, non-parametric Bayesian networks can capture the relationships between software components and their failure behaviors, helping to identify critical components that affect overall system reliability. Widely used in fields such as machine learning and reliability engineering, these models provide a flexible framework for representing complex systems, particularly when failure behavior is influenced by multiple interacting factors. Overall, non-parametric software reliability models offer a versatile, data-driven approach to analyzing and predicting software reliability. By avoiding strict parametric assumptions, they can adapt closely to observed failure data, making them suitable for a wide variety of applications. Techniques such as the Kaplan-Meier estimator, Nelson-Aalen estimator, Bayesian non-parametric models, and kernel density estimation each bring unique strengths and use cases. These models are particularly valuable in complex and dynamic environments where software failure behavior is not well understood or where failure data is highly variable. They equip reliability engineers and software developers with powerful tools to assess and improve system reliability accurately. By leveraging these approaches, organizations can achieve better insights into software failure patterns, make informed decisions to enhance reliability, and ultimately deliver higher-quality software products.

1.4.3 Hybrid Software Reliability Model

The Hybrid SRM is an advanced approach that integrates different modeling techniques, both stochastic and deterministic, to assess and forecast the reliability of software systems across various phases of development and operational use. This model combines traditional reliability models like Jelinski-Moranda and Goel-Okumoto with newer, machine learning-based or data-driven models to account for diverse failure behaviors during the software testing phase and post-release operational failures. By considering dynamic factors such as fault detection and introduction rates, the hybrid model improves the accuracy of reliability predictions over time. The integration of multiple failure modes and varying failure rates throughout the software lifecycle makes this approach versatile, catering to systems that experience frequent updates or those with minimal post-deployment changes. Additionally, it incorporates usage intensity, environmental conditions, and maintenance activities to offer a more comprehensive view of system reliability. This flexibility makes the hybrid model beneficial for both developers and stakeholders, allowing for better decision-making in software releases, maintenance schedules, and overall system improvements. It also ensures continuous reliability monitoring by leveraging data from operational environments, enhancing the model's precision with time.

Hybrid models combining ML techniques and traditional reliability models have been further developed to refine SRPs. Neural networks, fuzzy logic, Bayesian networks, genetic algorithms and Markov chains among others, are used to model complex relationships in failure data, allowing for more reliable predictions. For instance, the Neural Network-Enhanced Software Reliability Growth Model merges NN with conventional reliability growth models, improving prediction accuracy by addressing fault detection and introduction rates [23]. Bayesian network-based models tackle uncertainties and dependencies in software systems, while Markov Chain Monte Carlo (MCMC) models account for uncertainties by sampling from the posterior distributions of reliability parameters [24]. Fuzzy logic models handle uncertainty in software assessments through linguistic variables, and genetic algorithms optimize parameters for enhanced prediction performance [25]. Further, hybrid approaches such as the Gamma Process with Weibull distribution effectively model fault detection variability, and machine learning methods like SVM and fault tree analysis refine reliability predictions [26]. Ensemble methods that combine various models, such as Bayesian networks, neural networks, and Markov chains, provide a comprehensive and more reliable estimation of software reliability.

The Deep Reliability Network, a deep learning model, offers an even more sophisticated approach by learning intricate relationships between software metrics and reliability [27]. Hybrid models also integrate expert knowledge, guiding machine learning processes with domain-specific rules, enhancing both accuracy and interpretability [28]. Emerging technologies like blockchain and the Internet of Things (IoT) are increasingly incorporated into hybrid models, improving the security and real-time dynamic adjustments of reliability estimates for distributed systems. For example, the Blockchain-Assisted Software Reliability Model uses blockchain's decentralization and immutability to securely store reliability data while Bayesian networks perform probabilistic modeling [29]. Additionally, IoT-based models adjust reliability estimates based on real-time environmental conditions and device usage patterns, addressing the challenges of reliability prediction in the IoT ecosystem [30]. The growing trend of incorporating explainable AI techniques in hybrid models aims to provide greater transparency by identifying key factors influencing reliability predictions, which is crucial for stakeholders [31]. As software systems evolve, specialized models for edge computing environments and defect prediction datasets are gaining importance. These models address the unique challenges posed by decentralized processing and resource limitations, predicting reliability more effectively in such environments [32]. Models that integrate Extreme Learning Machines, Artificial NN and Ensemble Learning with Jaya optimization are increasingly utilized, alongside time-series models like SARIMA, to predict software reliability [33]. These advancements contribute significantly to improving the accuracy, flexibility, and interpretability of SRPs, making them applicable to both traditional and modern software systems, as well as complex environments like edge computing and IoT. As software systems become more complex and larger in scale, hybrid models remain valuable, providing developers and stakeholders with practical tools and insights to better manage software reliability.

1.5 Machine learning techniques used in our work

SRP is critical in ensuring the dependable performance of software systems, especially in domains where failures can have severe consequences. Various ML techniques have been applied to improve the performance of these predictions. They use historical data to learn complex patterns that traditional statistical methods may overlook. Here's an overview of why and how different ML techniques are applied in this domain. Firstly, regression models are commonly used for SRP. Linear regression and its more advanced counterparts, such as Regression trees, Support vector regression (SVR) and model the relationship between software metrics (like lines of code and past failure data and complexity measures) and reliability outcomes. These methods are particularly valued for their interpretability and simplicity, allowing practitioners to understand how different factors contribute to reliability. For instance, [34] highlighted the efficacy of multiple linear regressions in predicting fault-prone modules by correlating software metrics with failure data. Classification techniques are widely used, particularly for binary reliability prediction tasks, with decision trees, Random forest (RF) and support vector machines being common choices. These methods categorize software components based on patterns learned from historical data, with RFs standing out for their robustness against overfitting and their ability to manage high-dimensional datasets, as demonstrated by [35] in predicting software defects using ensemble learning methods.

Deep learning and NN models have demonstrated considerable potential in handling the complexity and non-linearity often present in software reliability data. These frameworks, including feed-forward neural network and convolutional neural networks are adept at learning intricate patterns and interactions between features. They are particularly useful in scenarios involving large datasets and where the relationships between variables are too complex for traditional models. Research in [36] found deep learning models perform better than traditional methods at predicting software defects because they can capture complex patterns and features within the data. Bayesian networks are also another powerful technique frequently used in SRP. These probabilistic graphical models represent the conditional dependencies between variables, providing a structured approach to integrate prior knowledge and manage uncertainty in predictions. This approach is beneficial when integrating expert knowledge with empirical data, as shown in the work by Fenton et al. [37], where Bayesian networks effectively modeled the uncertainty in software reliability assessments. Clustering techniques like hierarchical clustering are also employed, particularly for exploratory data analysis and feature selection. These methods cluster similar data points, aiding in the identification of patterns and outliers in software metrics, which can be crucial for refining predictive models. In [38] illustrated the use of clustering in improving the performance of defect prediction models by effectively handling heterogeneous data sets.

Finally, ensemble methods such as bagging, boosting and stacking integrate multiple learning algorithms to enhance predictive performance. By combining diverse models, these methods capitalize on their individual strengths while minimizing weaknesses. For instance, AdaBoost and Gradient Boosting Machines have been effectively utilized to improve the accuracy and robustness of SRP, as demonstrated in the benchmarking study by [39] on various ML techniques for defect prediction. In summary, the wide range of ML approaches used in SRP highlights both the complexity of the problem and the necessity for adaptable and high-performing models. Each technique provides distinct benefits, ranging from the clarity of regression models to the powerful representation learning of neural networks, and their integration through ensemble strategies further strengthens predictive capability. Together, these methods play a key role in building reliable and effective software systems that support modern technological advancements.

1.5.1 Support Vector Machines

Support Vector Machines (SVMs) are widely recognized as a powerful and flexible technique for SRP because of their capacity to handle high-dimensional data and build robust frameworks for both classification and regression tasks. SVMs operate by identifying the best hyperplane that maximizes the separation between classes in the feature space. In the context of software reliability, this typically involves distinguishing between fault-prone and non-fault-prone software modules, making SVMs particularly effective for binary classification problems. A major advantage of SVMs in SRP lies from their capability to manage extensive and complex datasets. Software projects often produce vast amounts of information, including code metrics, historical fault data, and other software attributes. SVMs perform well in such scenarios because they can efficiently manage a high number of features and maintain good performance even when there are more features than data points. This characteristic is essential for accurately predicting software reliability, as the relationships among various metrics and fault proneness are often nonlinear and multidimensional.

In practical applications, SVMs are implemented through a structured process that begins with data preprocessing, including feature selection and normalization, to make sure that all features have an equal influence on the decision-making process. The next step involves training the SVM model using labeled datasets where the fault status of each module is known. During training, the algorithm identifies support vectors, which represent the critical points that determine the decision boundary, and adjusts the hyperplane to maximize the separation between classes, improving the model's generalization to unseen data. Several studies have confirmed the effectiveness of SVMs in SRP. For example, [40] compared the performance of multiple ML techniques for SDP and found that SVMs consistently achieved strong results across diverse datasets. Their capability to accurately classify software modules as fault or non-fault-prone, even in the presence of imbalanced data, is a significant strength. This resilience to class imbalance is particularly valuable in SRP, where faulty modules are usually far fewer than non-faulty ones.

SVMs can be further enhanced through kernel functions, which enable the algorithm to work in a higher-dimensional space without directly computing the data coordinates in that space. This "kernel trick" enables SVMs to capture complex, non-linear relationships between features. Common kernels used in SRP include the radial basis function (RBF) and polynomial kernels. These transformations make it easier for the SVM to identify a hyperplane that clearly separates the classes. As highlighted in [41], kernel-based SVMs improve prediction accuracy by effectively handling the non-linearity present in software defect data. SVMs also offer a mechanism to balance model complexity and prediction accuracy through the regularization parameter. This parameter manages the trade-off between minimizing training error and reducing testing error, allowing the model to be fine-tuned according to the specific requirements of the software reliability task. In summary, SVMs are a vital tool for SRP due to their ability to manage high-dimensional, complex datasets and perform well in binary classification tasks. By combining the capability to find optimal hyperplanes with kernel functions to handle non-linear relationships, SVMs provide robust and accurate predictions of software reliability. Studies consistently demonstrate that SVMs are among the top-performing techniques for defect prediction, making them an essential resource for ensuring the reliability and quality of software systems.

1.5.2 Extreme Learning Machine-Based Methods

Extreme Learning Machines (ELMs) have become a notable method in SRP because of their ability to efficiently handle complex relationships and large datasets among software metrics. ELMs are a type of feedforward neural network in which the hidden layer parameters are randomly assigned and fixed, so only the output weights need to be learned. This approach leads to significant reductions in training time while maintaining high predictive accuracy, making ELMs particularly attractive for software reliability tasks. ELMs are employed in SRP to address the challenges of traditional ML methods that often struggle with the computational burden and scalability issues. Software systems generate extensive data from code metrics, historical faults, and operational profiles. ELMs excel in this environment by rapidly learning from these large and complex datasets without the iterative tuning required in conventional neural networks. This rapid learning is achieved through the unique structure of ELMs, where the hidden layer's parameters do not require tuning, thus significantly speeding up the training process.

The process of applying ELMs in SRP starts with data preprocessing, which involves feature extraction, normalization, and selection. This step ensures the input data is properly formatted for the ELM to process. Once the data is prepared, it is introduced into the ELM where the hidden layer neurons are initialized with random weights and biases. The core benefit here is that this initialization does not require adjustment, which enables the ELM to completely bypass the time consuming iterative training phase typical of traditional neural networks. Within the context of software reliability, ELMs are employed to model the connection between the probability of faults and software metrics. For example, by analyzing features like code complexity, historical defect data, and other relevant factors, ELMs can predict whether a software module is likely to be fault prone. This prediction aids in identifying crucial software areas needing more rigorous testing or refactoring, thereby improving overall software reliability. Studies confirm the effectiveness of ELMs in SRP [42] demonstrated that ELMs offer superior performance compared to traditional NN and SVM concerning both accuracy and training speed. That study highlighted the ELM's ability to efficiently handle large scale datasets, making them well suited for real time reliability prediction tasks. Similarly, ELM-based models, as reported in [43], achieved high accuracy in predicting software defects, outperforming several other machine learning techniques. Moreover, the robustness of ELMs in handling noisy and imbalanced data is another significant advantage, since software reliability datasets often include noise and class imbalances due to the diverse nature of software development and operational conditions. ELMs, with their inherent capacity to generalize well from noisy data, provide reliable predictions even in such challenging conditions. This robustness is further strengthened by the ELM's capacity to learn from diverse data while avoiding overfitting, as the random initialization of hidden nodes promotes diverse feature representation. Furthermore, the scalability of ELMs makes them ideal for continuous integration and deployment environments where software is frequently updated and rapid reliability assessment is crucial. The quick training time of ELMs ensures that they can be retrained with new data as software evolves, providing up-to-date reliability predictions without significant computational overhead. In conclusion, Extreme Learning Machines are a powerful tool in SRP due to their rapid training capability, scalability, and robustness against noisy and imbalanced data. By efficiently learning complex relationships among software metrics, ELMs provide accurate and timely predictions of software faults, which are essential for maintaining high software reliability.

Its architecture resembles a single-layer feedforward network (SLFN) but with notable differences. The output layer weights are computed analytically without using iterative methods like backpropagation, while the input layer weights are randomly assigned and remain unchanged. The activation function of the output layer yields a linear model; in this manner, a hidden layer of N neurons can be used to depict the architecture of an ELM. Input weights and hidden bias are produced at random, and the activation function is g(x) in order to learn N distinct arbitrary samplesx_i, t_i.

Where x_i= $[x_{i1}, x_{i2}, \dots\dots, x_{in}]^T \in R^m$ and $t_i = [t_{i1}, t_{i2}, \dots\dots, t_{in}]^T \in R^m$

The mathematical representation of the ELM is as follows:

$$\sum_{i=1}^{\underline{N}} \beta_i g(w_i . x_j + b_i) = o_j, \quad j = 1, \dots\dots, N, \tag{1.1}$$

where N is the total number of training samples and $\underline{N}$ is the total number of neurons in the hidden layer, and $\beta_i = [b_{i1}, b_{i2}, \dots\dots, b_{im}]^T$ stands for the weight vector that connects the i-th hidden layer neuron to neurons in the output layer, g(.) is the activation function, and $w_i = [w_{i1}, w_{i2}, \dots\dots, w_{in}]^T$T stands for the weight vector connecting the input layer neurons and the j-th hidden layer neuron; $x_j$stands for each unique sample; and b_j stands for the bias of the j-th hidden layer neuron. In order to perform error training equal to zero or to make the network outputs identical to the predicted outcomes, there must be b_i.

$$\sum_{i=1}^{\underline{N}} \beta_i g(w_i . x_j + b_i) = t_j, \quad j = 1, \dots\dots, N, \tag{1.2}$$

Where, in reference to the $x_j$sample input, t_j are the outputs that the network anticipates? The following equations are a compact representation of the previous N equations:

$$H\beta = T$$

$$\text{Where } H = \begin{bmatrix} g(w_i . x_j + b_1) & \cdots & g(w_{\overline{N}} . x_j + b_{\overline{N}}) \\ \vdots & \ddots & \vdots \\ g(w_i . x_N + b_1) & \cdots & g(w_{\overline{N}} . x_j + b_{\overline{N}}) \end{bmatrix}_{NX\overline{N}} \tag{1.3}$$

$$\beta = \begin{bmatrix} \beta_1^T \\ \cdot \\ \cdot \\ \cdot \\ \beta_{\bar{N}}^T \end{bmatrix}_{\bar{N} X m} \quad \text{And} \quad T = \begin{bmatrix} t_1^T \\ \cdot \\ \cdot \\ \cdot \\ t_{\bar{N}}^T \end{bmatrix}_{\bar{N} X m}$$

The preceding **H** is referred to as the output matrix of the neural network's hidden layer, and the ***ith*** column of **H** represents the i-th hidden layer neuron output vector corresponding to the entries$x_1, x_2, \dots \dots, x_N$. The ELM model is what we apply in this investigation. There are variables that, in the majority of cases, have a considerable impact on how well machine learning approaches operate. In the equations that follow, N equations are written concisely. For our experiment, we used the following parameters: alpha = 1.0, n_hidden = 5, activation ='sigmoid' and rbf_width = 0.1.

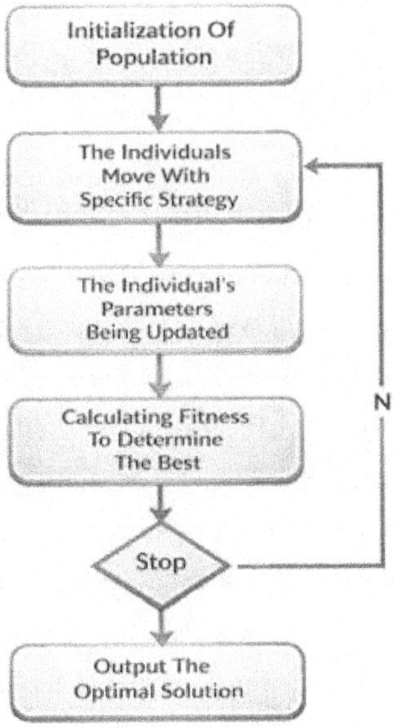

Fig. 1.4 ELM flowchart

1.5.3 Ensemble Learning

Ensemble learning has become increasingly important in SRP because it combines multiple ML models to deliver more accurate and reliable results. These methods bring together several base models, known as weak learners, to create a stronger overall predictor. One of the main benefits of ensemble approaches is that they reduce overfitting and improve generalization by taking advantage of the differences between individual models. Common techniques include bagging, boosting, and stacking. Bagging works by training multiple instances of the same algorithm on different subsets of the data and then combining their predictions, usually by averaging for regression or majority voting for classification. RFs, which are an extension of bagging applied to decision trees, are especially effective in software reliability tasks. By training many decision trees on different parts of the data and averaging their predictions, RFs reduce variance, improve stability, and produce more reliable outcomes. Studies like [41] show that RFs often outperform single classifiers in predicting software defects because of their robustness and ability to handle large, complex datasets. Boosting takes a different approach by training weak learners sequentially, with each new model focusing on correcting the mistakes of the previous ones, further enhancing predictive performance.

The concept is to fix the mistakes made by the earlier models by giving more weight to the misclassified instances. Gradient Boosting and AdaBoost machines are well-known boosting algorithms used in SRP. These methods enhance the predictive accuracy by progressively minimizing the prediction errors. For instance, [44] found that boosting techniques, particularly GBMs, significantly improved defect prediction performance by efficiently capturing complex structures within the dataset that individual models might overlook. Stacking, also called layered generalization, employs an alternative strategy by integrating several models through a meta-learner. In this technique, foundational models are initially trained on the dataset, and their outputs are subsequently fed into a meta-learner, which generates the ultimate prediction. This method leverages the strengths of diverse models and often improves performance by enabling the meta-learner to determine the best way to combine the outputs of the base models. As demonstrated in [45], stacking various ML models, including SVM, Decision trees and neural networks, and can enhance SRP accuracy by effectively integrating their individual predictions. Ensemble learning methods are particularly valuable in SRP due to the complexity and variability of software systems. Software metrics, fault data, and operational profiles often exhibit intricate and non-linear relationships that single models struggle to capture comprehensively. By combining multiple models, ensemble methods can better capture these relationships and provide more reliable predictions. Moreover, ensemble techniques are well-suited for handling imbalanced datasets, a common challenge in SRP, where defective modules are often far fewer than non-defective ones. Ensemble methods [46] can balance the bias-variance trade-off more effectively, resulting in more consistent and precise predictions. Furthermore, ensemble learning methods are highly scalable and can be adapted to various contexts within software engineering. They can be integrated into continuous integration and deployment pipelines, where real-time reliability predictions are crucial for maintaining software quality. The scalability of ensemble methods ensures that they can handle large datasets and evolving software metrics, rendering them well-suited for dynamic and complex software environments. In conclusion, ensemble learning-based methods serve an essential role in SRP by integrating the capabilities of multiple models to attain greater accuracy and resilience. Ensemble learning techniques efficiently tackle the challenges arising from variability and complexity of software systems.

1.5.4 Artificial Neural Networks

Artificial Neural Networks (ANNs) are a type ML models inspired by the functioning and structure of the human brain are designed to recognize patterns and make predictions from input data, making them especially valuable for SRP. ANNs consist of interconnected neurons organized into an input layer, an output layer, and one or more hidden layers.. Each neuron processes incoming signals, applies corresponding weights, and transmits the results through an activation function. The learning process involves updating the weights through backpropagation in conjunction with optimization algorithms like gradient descent. In SRP, ANNs are trained using historical failure data, software metrics, and environmental factors to predict the likelihood of future system failures. ANNs excel in modeling both linear and non-linear relationships, which is critical for capturing the complex interactions in software systems. By learning from large datasets, ANNs can recognize intricate patterns related to software faults and failures, helping predict reliability over time [47]. Deep neural networks, a more advanced form of ANNs, enhance this capability by learning from even larger datasets, making them effective in handling more complex and high-dimensional reliability prediction tasks. ANNs offer a significant advantage in software reliability by continuously refining predictions based on new data, improving forecasting accuracy, and identifying potential failure points. Despite requiring substantial computational resources and large datasets for training, ANNs provide valuable insights into system reliability, which is crucial for proactive maintenance and optimization in software engineering. Although they are sometimes seen as "black-box" models, the benefits they bring in predicting software reliability make them a powerful tool in modern software development and maintenance.

ANNs are widely used in SRP because of their ability to model non-linear relationships and complex within the software data. During training, layers of interconnected neurons process input data and gradually learn complex patterns. They are particularly effective in handling large datasets and diverse software metrics, including code complexity measures, historical fault data, and usage patterns. The training process involves adjusting the weights of connections between neurons based on prediction errors, allowing the network to improve accuracy over time. In SRP, ANNs are commonly employed to estimate the likelihood of faults or failures in software modules. The process starts with data preprocessing, which involves standardizing the dividing the dataset and input features into training and testing subsets. The normalized data is then fed into the ANN [48], where it passes through multiple hidden layers before producing an output that represents the predicted reliability of the software. One of the main strengths of ANNs lies in their capability to automatically learn and derive meaningful features from raw data, eliminating the need for manual feature engineering. This makes them particularly suitable for complex and high-dimensional datasets common in software engineering. For example, [49] demonstrated that ANNs could effectively predict software defects by learning from various metrics and historical failure data, outperforming traditional statistical approaches. ANNs can also be integrated with other ML techniques to boost predictive performance. Hybrid frameworks that merge ANNs with methods such as fuzzy logic or genetic algorithms have demonstrated improved accuracy and robustness in SRPs. Additionally, [50] illustrated that combining ANNs with ensemble methods yielded better prediction results than using ANNs alone. Overall, numerous studies have consistently confirmed the effectiveness of ANNs in SRP.

1.5.5 Evolutionary Optimization Techniques

Modeled on natural selection and genetic processes, evolutionary optimization methods have become highly effective tools for solving complex optimization problems. Examples of these methods are evolutionary strategies, genetic algorithms, differential evolution, ant colony optimization and particle swarm optimization all of which mimic evolutionary or natural processes to identify optimal solutions within a given problem domain. Across successive generations, genetic algorithms evolve a population of candidate solutions, assessing each one with a fitness function and generating new solutions through genetic operations such as crossover and mutation. Evolutionary strategies focus on adapting the variance of the search distribution to effectively explore promising areas of the solution space. Differential evolution improves candidate solutions iteratively by combining information from multiple candidates to create new ones. Replicating collective behaviors observed in nature, such as bird flocking or fish schooling, particle swarm optimization updates each solution's position based on its own experience and the best solution found by neighboring solutions. Ant colony optimization, inspired by ants' foraging behavior, uses artificial ants that leave pheromone trails to mark promising solutions and follow trails laid by others. These techniques have been effectively applied in fields like engineering design, finance, data mining, and logistics, demonstrating their ability to navigate complex, multi-dimensional search spaces and identify near optimal solutions.

Optimization itself is a fundamental concept in mathematics and computer science, involving the process of finding the best solution from a set of feasible alternatives. It is widely applicable across disciplines such as economics, engineering, ML and operations research [51]. The objective of optimization is to maximize or minimize a function while satisfying certain constraints. Various techniques exist, ranging from classical approaches like linear programming and gradient descent to advanced methods including evolutionary algorithms and stochastic optimization. Linear programming addresses problems with linear objective functions and constraints, while gradient descent, one of the earliest iterative optimization algorithms, minimizes differentiable functions. Populations of candidate solutions are evolved by evolutionary algorithms over multiple generations to reach optimal or near-optimal solutions. Stochastic optimization techniques, including simulated annealing and genetic algorithms, probabilistically explore the search space to locate global optima. These diverse methods cater to a wide range of problem complexities and are critical for advancing scientific research, technological development, and decision-making across multiple domains.

1.5.6 Jaya Optimization

Jaya Optimization (JAYA) is a relatively new optimization algorithm designed as a simple yet powerful approach for solving optimization problems. Unlike traditional techniques, Based on the principle of iterative improvement, JAYA [52] does not use algorithm-specific parameters or operators such as mutation, crossover, or selection. In each iteration, it evaluates the current solutions to determine the best and worst, and then updates all solutions by shifting them closer to the best and away from the worst. This approach allows improvement without the need for complex parameter tuning or control mechanisms. JAYA's simplicity and efficiency make it especially well-suited for complex or high-dimensional search spaces. Research has demonstrated that, in terms of convergence speed and solution quality, JAYA can surpass many other optimization algorithms across diverse real-world applications. Both JAYA and Particle Swarm Optimization (PSO) provide effective optimization strategies, each with distinct strengths, making them valuable for solving a wide variety of problems. Originally developed to solve both constrained and unconstrained optimization problems, the JAYA algorithm derives its name from Sanskrit, meaning "victory." Inspired by the natural principle of "survival of the fittest," this population-based metaheuristic integrates elements of both evolutionary and swarm-based methods. The algorithm steers solutions toward the globally best outcomes while moving them away from the worst, effectively pursuing success and avoiding failure. Its main advantages over other population-based approaches include simplicity, ease of implementation, and independence from algorithm-specific parameters such as population size or maximum iterations. The six procedural steps for the JAYA algorithm are described in this overview article as a fresh presentation. These operational procedures can make using this method simpler for academics studying optimisation techniques. The flowchart in fig.1.5 illustrates the JAYA algorithm's steps-by-step process. Algorithm 1 also provides the JAYA algorithm's pseudocode. The following phases cover the JAYA algorithm's process in detail:

Step 1: Set the JAYA method and the optimisation problem's parameters to their initial values. In the opening step of the run, the JAYA algorithm's parameters are set. The JAYA algorithm is interesting in that it has no control parameters. Population size N and iteration numbers T are the only two algorithmic parameters. The constrained problem is typically represented in the optimisation context as follows:

$$minf(x)$$

$$g_j(x) = c_j \qquad \forall j = (1,2, \dots \dots ..n) \tag{1.4}$$

$$h_k(x) \leq d_k \qquad \forall k = (1,2, \dots \dots ..m) \tag{1.5}$$

$x = (x_1, x_2, \dots \dots \dots, x_d)$ Where *f(x)* is the objective function used to determine the solution's fitness value. $x_i$is a decision variable that is given a value from the lower and upper bound range if and only if$x_i \in [X_i^{min}, X_i^{max}]$. The jth and ***k*** inequality restrictions are denoted by the symbols g_j and h_k, respectively. Typically, for a benchmark dataset, the problem variables, dimensions, and relevant data are extracted.

Step 2: Building the JAYA's initial population.

The JAYA Memory (JM) stores the initial solutions, or population, of the algorithm after they are generated. In Eq. 2, N represents the number of solutions, and D denotes the solution dimension, it is important to keep in mind that the JM is an augmented matrix of size ***N X D***. The conventional formula for the answer is

$$JM_{i_j} = X_j^{min} + \left(X_j^{min} - X_j^{max}\right) X\, rnd, \forall i \in (1,2, \dots \dots, N) \wedge \forall j \in (1,2, \dots \dots ., D). \tag{1.6}$$

A uniform function called "rnd" creates random numbers between "0" and "1" at random.

JM = $[x_1^1\ x_2^1\ \cdots\ x_D^1\ x_1^2\ x_2^2\ \cdots\ x_D^2\ \vdots \vdots\ \cdots\ \vdots\ x_1^N\ x_2^N\ \cdots\ x_D^N\ ][f(x^1)\ f(x^2)\ \vdots\ f(x^N)\ ]$ (1.7)

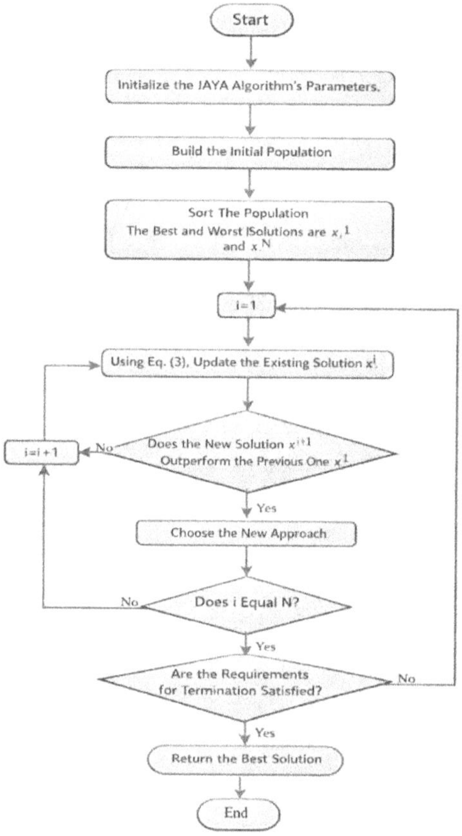

Fig. 1.5 Jaya algorithm flowchart

The JM solutions are arranged in ascending order depending on the values of their objective functions, along with the objective function $f(x_i)$for each solution. The best answer is x^1, while the worst solution is x^N as a result.

Step 3: JAYA process, from one iteration to the next, all solutions in the JM undergo changes in their decision variables using the JAYA operator defined in Eq. 3.

$$x_j'^{i} = x_j^i + r_1 * \left(x_j^1 - |x_j^i|\right) - r_2 * \left(x_j^N - |x_j^i|\right) \quad (1.8)$$

The improved solution, x'^i has replaced the previous one, x_j^i. The modified value of the decision value x_j^i, is $x_j'^i$. r_1 and r_2 are two uniform functions that produce random values between [0, 1]. The decision variable in the best solution is, x^1, j while the decision variable in the worst solution isx^n, j. In the JAYA algorithm, diversity control is determined by the distances between the decision variables of the current solution and those of both the best and worst solutions. Higher exploitation results from closer proximity, whereas higher exploration results from greater distance.

Step 4: Update JM, every iteration will result in an update to the JM solutions. Calculations are made to determine the objective function value of the new solution. If so, $f(x'^i) \leq f(x^i)$ then the new solution x'^i will take the place of the current solution x^i. There will be N repetitions of this process.

Step 5: Apply the stopping rule. The JAYA algorithm proceeds through Steps 3 and 4 repeatedly until the halting condition is satisfied, which is sometimes set as the maximum number of iterations, T.

The JAYA algorithm's pseudocode
Set the parameters (N, T, etc.) for the Jaya algorithm and the optimisation problem.
Create a population of N solutions at random.
Sort the population using the best and worst options, respectively (x^1 *and* x^N).
$t = 1$
$while(t \leq T)\ do$
$for\ i = 1, \ldots\ldots, N\ do$
$for\ j = 1, \ldots\ldots, D\ do$
$Set\ r_1 \in [0,1]$
$Set\ r_2 \in [0,1]$
$x_j'^i = x_j^i + r1 * (x_j^1 - |x_j^i|) - r2 * (x_j^N - |x_j^i|)$
$end\ for$
$if\ f(x'^i) \leq f(x^i)\ then$
$x^i = x'^i \quad \{updated\ process\}$
$end\ if$
$end\ for$
$t = t + 1$
$end\ while$

1.5.7 Synthetic Minority Oversampling Technique

Synthetic Minority Oversampling Technique (SMOTE) was developed as an effective approach to tackle the common problem of class imbalance in supervised learning, especially in classification tasks. In numerous real-world datasets [53], the minority class is heavily underrepresented relative to the majority class, which can result in biased classifiers that favor the majority and perform inadequately on the minority class. SMOTE improves the minority class distribution by generating new synthetic samples rather than simply duplicating existing minority instances, as is done in basic oversampling methods. This approach enhances the classifier's ability to generalize. The key principle of SMOTE involves creating synthetic minority samples through interpolation between existing minority instances and their nearest neighbors in the feature space, effectively enriching the dataset and addressing class imbalance. Formally, let us denote the minority class dataset as$D_{minority} = \{x_1, x_2, \ldots\ldots, x_N\}$, where each $x_i \in R^d$ represents a feature vector with d dimensions, and N is the total number of minority samples. For each minority sample x_i, SMOTE identifies its k-nearst neighbors within the minority class using a distance metric, typically the Euclidean distance:$dist(x_i, x_j) = \sqrt{\sum_{m=1}^{d}(x_i^{(m)} - x_j^{(m)})^2}$. Once the neighbors are found, the algorithm randomly selects one neighbor x_{zi} for each synthetic sample to be generated and the new synthetic sample to be generated.

The new synthetic sample x_{new} is then created using the equation $x_{new} = x_i + \lambda(x_{zi} - x_i),\ where\ \lambda \in [0,1]$ is a random scalar drawn from a uniform distribution. This equation represents a convex combination of $x_i\ and\ x_{zi,}$ ensuring that the synthetic sample lies somewhere along the line segment connecting these two points. Geometrically, this process "fills in" the gaps between sparse minority class points in the feature space, increasing their density and diversity without simply replicating the same data points. The choice of k, commonly set to 5, balances the variety of synthetic samples while preventing overlap with majority class regions. The number of synthetic samples generated depends on the desired oversampling percentage, which is often calculated based on the imbalance ratio. By augmenting the minority class with synthetic points, SMOTE improves the training dataset's balance, helping classifiers avoid bias toward the majority class and achieve better performance on minority examples. The technique preserves the underlying structure of the minority class since the new points are interpolations between real samples rather than random noise, which aids in building a more generalizable model. However, SMOTE has limitations; it does not explicitly consider the majority class distribution, which sometimes results in synthetic samples near class boundaries, potentially introducing noise or class overlap. Additionally, when the minority class instances are too sparse or scattered, SMOTE's interpolations may not produce meaningful new examples. Despite these limitations, SMOTE continue to be a widely used and effective technique in practice.

1.6 Relation between Software reliability prediction with Software defect prediction and Software fault prediction

Software reliability prediction, Software defect prediction, and Software fault prediction are closely related and complementary processes that collectively aim to improve software quality by anticipating and mitigating potential issues. SDP focuses on identifying parts of the code most likely to contain defects, based on historical defect data, code metrics, and complexity factors. It helps developers target areas that need more rigorous testing or debugging. Software fault prediction, on the other hand, looks at potential faults in the system, considering factors like error-prone modules, failure modes, and operational conditions. It estimates where and when faults might occur during the software's operation, helping to focus preventive measures on high-risk areas. SRP builds on both defect and fault prediction by estimating the system's overall reliability over time, including the likelihood of system failures, fault detection rates, and the system's performance during and after deployment. While defect prediction highlights areas prone to faults before deployment, fault prediction focuses on the risk of failures occurring during operation, and reliability prediction provides an overall estimate of how the system will perform as failures accumulate over time. By integrating insights from all three, software engineers can better prioritize testing, code improvements, and maintenance activities, leading to more robust, reliable, and high-quality software systems. Hybrid models that combine these predictive techniques often utilizing machine learning algorithms allow for continuous refinement of predictions, enabling more accurate forecasting of software behavior, minimizing risks, and improving decision-making throughout the software lifecycle.

1.7 Research Motivation

The motivation for employing ML models in SRP stems from the critical need to enhance software quality assurance processes. Conventional reliability prediction methods typically rely on heuristic rules, expert judgment, or simple statistical models, which often struggle to capture the complex dependencies and dynamic behaviors present in modern software systems. By using advanced machine learning techniques such as supervised learning, ensemble approaches, and deep learning, researchers aim to develop more accurate and robust predictive models that can detect potential faults and failures with greater precision.

Machine learning-based approaches enable the analysis of extensive historical datasets, incorporating diverse sources such as code complexity metrics, defect reports, execution traces, and system logs. These models can uncover latent patterns and correlations that influence software reliability, offering data-driven insights that surpass conventional prediction techniques. Furthermore, machine learning models possess the capacity for continuous learning and adaptive improvement, refining their predictive capabilities over time as they process additional data and receive feedback.

The structure of this thesis is organized to systematically examine the integration of ML in SRP. It starts with an introduction to the core concepts of software reliability and the essential role of predictive modeling in maintaining software quality and dependability. This is followed by a comprehensive literature review that critically evaluates existing SRP methodologies, emphasizing their strengths, weaknesses, and potential areas for improvement.

Subsequently, the thesis delves into the theoretical underpinnings of ML algorithms relevant to SRP, discussing techniques such as SVM, NN, decision trees, and ensemble learning methods. The methodology section outlines the systematic approach used to develop and evaluate machine learning models, covering data collection and preprocessing, feature selection and engineering, model training and validation, and performance evaluation using standard metrics. It also addresses important aspects such as model interpretability, scalability, and robustness to ensure that the proposed models are practically applicable.

The experimental results section presents empirical findings from applying machine learning models to real-world software datasets. This includes a performance analysis of the models, comparative assessments against conventional prediction methods, and discussions on the practical implications of the results for software quality assurance. Finally, the thesis concludes with a synthesis of key findings, contributions to the field, study limitations, and recommendations for future research directions.

This thesis aims to offer a comprehensive exploration of how ML can be applied in SRP, emphasizing its potential to enhance software quality assurance practices. It highlights the advantages of using machine learning, examines the associated challenges, and provides insights into the ways these techniques can contribute to more effective and reliable software reliability prediction.

1.8 Research Objectives

This research has proposed novel methodologies to enhance the accuracy and reliability of SRP models. The key objectives achieved in this study are as follows:

- **Development of Hybrid Machine Learning Models for SRP**

The study designed and implemented hybrid ML models that integrate multiple learning techniques to improve predictive accuracy. These models were further optimized through advanced optimization algorithms to enhance parameter tuning and feature selection processes. The proposed models demonstrated both high performance and computational efficiency, effectively addressing key challenges in SRP.

- **Comparative Performance Evaluation of Hybrid Models**

The proposed hybrid models were evaluated extensively using both real-world and benchmark datasets to assess their effectiveness. A thorough performance comparison was carried out against traditional statistical models and standalone machine learning approaches. Results across multiple evaluation metrics demonstrated the superior accuracy, reliability, and adaptability of the hybrid models in a variety of software reliability scenarios.

- **Impact Analysis of Feature Selection and Extraction on Model Performance**

The study examined how feature selection and extraction techniques can enhance the accuracy and computational efficiency of SRP models. By identifying and utilizing the most relevant predictive features, the research improved model performance while minimizing computational overhead. This strategy ensured that the hybrid models delivered both high accuracy and operational efficiency.

- **Integration of Time-Series Forecasting with Machine Learning**

Time-series forecasting techniques were explored to analyze temporal dependencies in software reliability data, focusing on identifying patterns in software failure occurrences. Additionally, time-series components were integrated with ML models to enhance predictive accuracy. This combined approach successfully leveraged the strengths of both methodologies, leading to more precise and reliable SRP models.

- **Optimization of Computational Efficiency and Generalizability**

The study optimized the training time and reduced the computational complexity of hybrid models while maintaining high predictive accuracy. Various configurations of hidden neurons were experimented with, and cross-validation techniques were employed to improve model efficiency. Furthermore, the models were validated across diverse software reliability datasets to ensure robustness and generalizability in real-world applications.

- **Contribution to Software Quality Assurance and Predictive Analytics**

The research provided actionable insights into software quality assurance and reliability improvement through predictive analytics. The findings demonstrated the practical benefits of hybrid machine learning models in software project management, equipping practitioners with data-driven tools for enhancing software development, maintenance, and reliability assessment processes.

This research has significantly contributed to the advancement of predictive analytics in software reliability engineering by developing innovative hybrid modeling techniques that improve accuracy, efficiency, and applicability in real-world scenarios.

1.9 Research Contribution

This thesis contributes significantly to the field of SRP by developing hybrid ML models that combine advanced techniques such as ELM, SVM, and SARIMA. By integrating the strengths of each method, the research enhances both prediction accuracy and model robustness. Optimization algorithms like Jaya are also employed to improve parameter tuning and feature selection, ensuring optimal model performance while minimizing computational overhead. Furthermore, the study explores the use of time-series forecasting methods, such as SARIMA, to capture temporal patterns in software failure data, providing valuable insights into the evolving dynamics of software reliability over time.

The thesis emphasizes the practical applicability of the proposed models by evaluating their performance using real-world and benchmark datasets. Comparative analyses are conducted against traditional statistical methods and standalone machine learning models, demonstrating the superiority of the hybrid approach in terms of accuracy, reliability, and adaptability. Furthermore, feature optimization is explored to identify the most relevant attributes, leading to more efficient and accurate prediction models. By experimenting with configurations such as hidden neurons and cross-validation techniques, the research ensures that the models maintain high prediction accuracy while minimizing computational complexity.

In addition to its technical contributions, this research advances software engineering practices by providing actionable insights for software quality assurance and reliability improvement. The proposed models are designed to be robust, generalizable, and practical for real-world software systems and projects. By showcasing the benefits of predictive analytics in software project management, the thesis highlights the value of hybrid machine learning models in enhancing software development and maintenance processes. This work not only contributes to the theoretical understanding of SRP but also equips practitioners with effective tools for improving software quality and reliability in industry.

1.10 Thesis Organisation

The thesis is organized into six chapters, as outlined below:

Chapter 1:

This chapter presents an overview of the research background, objectives, and key contributions. It begins with an introduction to software reliability, highlighting its importance, the factors influencing it, measurement methods, and strategies for improvement. The chapter then discusses various types of software reliability models, including parametric, non-parametric, and hybrid approaches, alongside a detailed examination of machine learning techniques such as support vector machines, extreme learning machines, ensemble learning, artificial neural networks, and evolutionary optimization methods like Jaya optimization. Additionally, it explores the connections between SRP, defect prediction, and fault prediction, and concludes with the research motivation, objectives, contributions, and a brief outline of the thesis structure.

Chapter 2:

This chapter critically examines existing research on software reliability models, focusing on parametric, non-parametric, and hybrid models. It explores the role of optimization algorithms in enhancing hybrid models and identifies research gaps, forming the foundation for the proposed methodologies.

Chapter 3:

This chapter introduces a hybrid model combining the JAYA optimization algorithm and the Extreme learning machine (ELM) classifier for SRP. It details the experimental setup, dataset, parameter descriptions, and performance evaluation metrics. The chapter presents the proposed feature selection model, followed by an analysis of results from the Promise and Java repositories, and a comparison with existing methods.

Chapter 4:

This chapter addresses the challenges of SRP in imbalanced and balanced datasets. It proposes a model using ensemble learning techniques on selected features. The chapter outlines the problem formulation, data preprocessing, model design, computation techniques, and performance criteria. It concludes with a discussion of results and challenges encountered during the study.

Chapter 5:

This chapter presents a hybrid ANN-SARIMA model enhanced by JAYA optimization for improved SRP. It describes the dataset, hyper parameter settings for the ANN, performance measures, and experimental setup. The results and discussions highlight the model's effectiveness and its comparison with existing approaches. Challenges faced during the development and implementations of the model are also addressed.

Chapter 6:

The final chapter summarizes the research contributions and findings of the thesis. It outlines the implications of the study for SRP and proposes directions for future research in this domain.

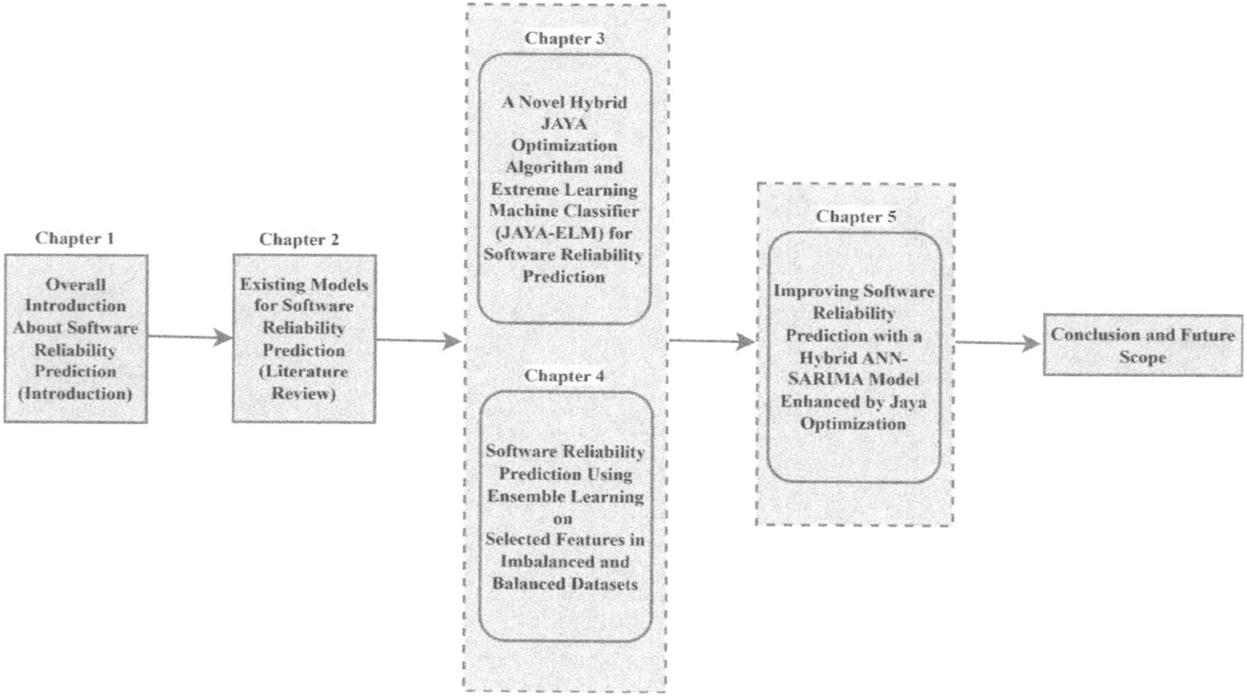

Fig. 1.6 Content flow of this research frame work

CHAPTER:2 Literature Review

2.1 A Comprehensive Review of Software Reliability Models

Software engineering is a field dedicated to a systematic, disciplined, and quantifiable approach to the operation, development and maintenance of software. Over the past decade, significant advancements and shifts have occurred, driven by evolving methodologies, technologies, and practices. Key developments in software engineering include the evolution of Agile methodologies, which emphasize collaboration, flexibility and iterative development processes, becoming the cornerstone of software development by promoting regular feedback and adaptation to changing requirements [54]. DevOps serves as a crucial collaborative framework that unites development and operations teams. It helps streamline the software delivery process, improving both speed and quality [55]. Another major trend is the shift from monolithic architectures to micro services, where applications are developed as a suite of small, independently deployable services, enhancing scalability, maintainability, and independent deployment [56].

Cloud computing has revolutionized software engineering by providing flexible, on-demand access to scalable resources and services, enabling rapid deployment, seamless scalability, and efficient application management. Platforms such as Microsoft Azure, AWS and Google Cloud have become integral to modern development [57]. Additionally, AI and ML are increasingly integrated into software engineering processes for tasks such as automated code generation, predictive analytics for software maintenance, and enhancing software testing [58]. The implementation of automated testing and CI/CD pipelines has become widespread, significantly improving the quality and Enhancing software delivery speed by continuously validating code changes and enabling the swift deployment of updates. finally, with the increasing prevalence of cyber threats and regulatory requirements, security and privacy have become paramount, leading to the integration of secure coding practices, comprehensive security testing, and Compliance with standards like the General data protection regulation [59].

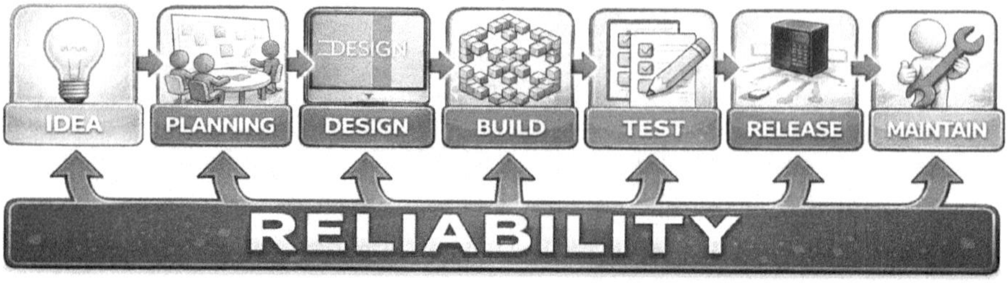

Fig. 2.1 Software development & reliability life cycle [60]

The SDLC [61] is a framework that describes the distinct stages of software development, supporting a structured and efficient methodology. Each phase has specific goals and deliverables, interconnected to create a cohesive process. The key phases of software development consist of requirement analysis, design, implementation, testing, deployment, and maintenance. In the requirement analysis stage, stakeholder expectations are gathered and documented to create a solid foundation and minimize scope changes. The design phase converts these requirements into a comprehensive blueprint, outlining the technical specifications and system architecture. In the implementation phase, developers create and integrate the source code through iterative cycles to meet design objectives, followed by the testing phase, which verifies functionality across multiple levels, including unit, integration, system, and user acceptance testing. Deployment entails delivering the final product to users, necessitating careful planning to guarantee a seamless transition from development to production. Maintenance follows, involving updates and improvements post-deployment to fix bugs, update features, and meet evolving user needs. Each phase is closely interrelated, with requirement analysis informing design, which guides implementation, verified by testing, leading to deployment, and followed by maintenance that revisits all phases as new issues and requirements emerge. Effective communication and documentation are crucial throughout the SDLC to ensure smooth transitions between phases and alignment with overall project goals [62].

The SDLC is intrinsically linked to software reliability, as each phase contributes to the robustness, performance, and dependability of the final product. Software reliability is the probability that a software system will operate according to its intended functions without encountering failures [63]. This discussion examines how different phases of the SDLC impact software reliability, supported by journal references. The requirement analysis phase is critical for establishing a clear and accurate understanding of what the software is supposed to achieve. Reliable software begins with well-defined requirements that encompass functional needs and non-functional requirements include as security, performance and reliability [64]. Inadequate or ambiguous requirements can lead to design flaws and implementation errors, ultimately affecting reliability. During the design phase, the architecture and detailed design specifications are created. Design decisions significantly affect software reliability, as a robust design can anticipate potential issues and incorporate fault-tolerance mechanisms [65]. Architectural patterns that promote modularity, such as micro services, can enhance reliability by isolating failures to individual components. The implementation phase involves translating design specifications into executable code.

Coding practices, adherence to standards, and the use of reliable libraries and frameworks play crucial roles in this phase. Approaches like pair programming, code reviews, and static analysis tools assist in detecting and addressing potential reliability issues early in the development cycle. Testing is paramount for verifying that the software meets its requirements and identifying defects before deployment [66]. Various testing strategies are employed to ensure the reliability. Automated testing frameworks can provide extensive coverage and detect regression issues that might compromise reliability. The deployment phase involves releasing the software to the user environment. Reliable deployment processes, including thorough release planning, rollback procedures, and real-time monitoring, are crucial for minimizing issues during this phase. Continuous Deployment (CD) practices can help ensure that new releases do not introduce reliability problems by incorporating automated testing and deployment pipelines [67]. Maintenance encompasses all post-deployment activities, including bug fixes, updates, and enhancements. Effective maintenance strategies ensure that reliability is sustained throughout the software's lifecycle. Practices such as regular updates, patch management, and ongoing monitoring help identify and address reliability issues that arise during usage. Each phase of the SDLC is interconnected and collectively contributes to software reliability. Requirements analysis lays the groundwork by defining reliability goals. The design phase translates these goals into a reliable architecture. Implementation ensures that coding practices uphold these design principles. Testing rigorously verifies that the implementation meets reliability standards.

Deployment ensures that the transition to the user environment does not compromise reliability, and maintenance sustains reliability through proactive management of issues [68]. By understanding and managing the interconnections between SDLC phases, software engineers can systematically enhance software reliability, ensuring that the final product performs consistently and dependably under specified conditions.

SRP aims to evaluate a software system's reliability by analyzing historical data, current development practices, and specific software characteristics. Here, Reliability refers to the probability that a software system will carry out its intended functions without failure for certain duration under specified conditions. Techniques for predicting software reliability typically employ statistical models, ML methods, and empirical data to estimate the probability of defects and failures [69]. These predictions are crucial for planning, resource allocation, and improving the software development process. SDP aims to detect the components of software that are most likely to have defects., typically using historical defect data, code metrics, and other relevant factors such as developer experience and code churn. Defect prediction models help prioritize testing efforts and improve software quality by targeting areas with a higher likelihood of defects. Software fault prediction is closely related to defect prediction but focuses more specifically on predicting the occurrences of faults (or bugs) within the software. Fault prediction models use similar data and techniques as defect prediction models, but they might also incorporate fault localization techniques and more detailed historical fault data to identify specific lines of code or modules where faults are likely to occur. SRP, defect prediction, and fault prediction are interrelated concepts that collectively contribute to improving software quality and reliability [70]. All three types of predictions rely on similar types of data, including historical defect and fault data, code metrics, and development process metrics. Techniques such as statistical analysis, machine learning, and empirical modeling are applied across all three domains, with approaches like logistic regression, decision trees, and NN commonly used to predict the reliability. By detecting potential defects and faults at an early stage, defect and fault prediction models enhance software reliability by directing developers' attention to the most high-risk areas. Predictions from defect and fault models can inform reliability models, as information on high-risk modules can be used to adjust reliability prediction models to reflect potential reliability issues more accurately. Effective defect and fault prediction contributes to better testing strategies and maintenance plans, enabling targeted testing and focused maintenance efforts, thereby supporting higher reliability. In summary, SRP, defect prediction, and fault prediction are complementary approaches that together strengthen the robustness and dependability of software systems. By utilizing these predictive methods, organizations can improve their development processes, produce higher-quality software, and maintain long-term reliability [71].

2.2 Parametric Software Reliability Models

Software reliability is a key quality metric in the software industry, offering developers and users insight into the potential number of faults within the software. As mentioned earlier, SRGM can be carried out using either parametric or non-parametric methods. Parametric models depend on specific assumptions made by researchers and commonly employ statistical techniques such as regression and non-homogeneous Poisson processes (NHPP). Over the years, numerous SRGMs have been introduced in the literature. For instance, one of the earliest and most widely used models applied maximum likelihood estimation to address parameter instability issues in the J&M model [72]. Another study proposed an error detection model, observing that the error detection curve followed an S-shaped pattern, which led to the development of the S-shaped growth model [73]. Additionally, a model based on the NHPP framework was suggested, assuming that undetected errors could be identified without resulting in software failures [74]. Additionally, a test-effort-based growth model was developed using a Weibull curve to represent the relationship between testing effort and time, based on the NHPP framework [75].

The goal of SRGMs is to define a stochastic process that characterizes software behavior concerning failures. This stochastic process can be applied to estimate software reliability, evaluate the system's current condition, and forecast future reliability. SRGMs are built on the assumption that as testing continues, system corrections and updates gradually reduce the failure rate and enhance reliability. Since the foundational research in this area, SRGMs have attracted extensive attention, leading to hundreds of studies and the development of over a hundred model variations [76]. These models are typically divided into two categories, time-between-failures models and failure-count models. The time-between-failures model was the first to emerge, while the earliest failure-count model was introduced later based on the Goel-Okumoto NHPP framework [77].

SRGMs are based on several underlying assumptions, some of which are debated for their realism. A fundamental assumption in SRGMs is that the time between failures is independent, meaning successive failure times are considered unrelated. This assumption remains valid only when test cases are randomly selected; however, in practical scenarios, systematic testing tends to create dependent test cases, thus breaching this assumption [78]. Another assumption is the immediate correction of detected faults, which is valid only if testing halts until the fault is fixed. In reality, testing often continues without correcting detected faults, which affects the fault detection rate. Furthermore, SRGMs assume that fixing a fault does not create new faults to ensure a steadily decreasing failure rate. In reality, however, fault corrections can often introduce additional faults. Some argue that newly introduced faults may minimally impact model results if they represent a small fraction of the fault population [79]. These assumptions remain environment-dependent. The application of time series ARIMA models was introduced to eliminate unrealistic assumptions and offered statistical proof that these models precisely represent the stochastic behavior of software failures [80].

The applicability of SRGMs poses another major challenge, since no single model can be applied universally. Various models must be tested and selected based on the specific development environment, a process requiring expert judgment and considerable time. The primary aim of SRGMs is to achieve predictability, which involves forecasting future reliability from the available data, such as time-between-failures or failure counts. For instance, one model may assume that the total number of software defects is initially fixed, with the defect detection rate proportional to the number of remaining undetected defects. Another model employs an NHPP to represent defect detection, assuming an exponential decay in which the software failure rate decreases exponentially as errors are identified and corrected over time [81]. Yet another model suggests that the defect detection rate declines logarithmically with execution time, indicating a slowing rate of failure discovery as testing continues [82]. Another model represents defect detection with an S-shaped curve, where the detection rate initially is slow, then accelerates, and finally decelerates, reflecting the testing process more realistically [83]. The Weibull model utilizes the Weibull distribution to describe the time to defect detection, providing flexibility to model different phases of defect detection behavior. Another model assumes defect detection follows an exponential decay, positing that the defect detection rate decreases over time as errors are gradually discovered and fixed [84].

Other models include a Bayesian inference-based model to predict software defects [85] and a model incorporating a change-point in defect detection rates to provide more accurate predictions [86]. The Crow-AMSAA model employs NHPP to track reliability growth over time as defects are detected and fixed. The Logarithmic Poisson Execution Time model and other parametric models like the Geometric Poisson, Gamma Poisson, Pareto, Inverse Gaussian, Exponential, Logistic, and Rayleigh models offer unique approaches to defect prediction [87]. Each has specific assumptions and applications depending on the testing phase and environment. However, many parametric SRGMs face limitations, such as unrealistic assumptions about the independence of failures, immediate fault correction, and the absence of new faults during debugging. In actual software development environments, these assumptions frequently do not apply [88]. Furthermore, the changing behavior of software during testing due to code modifications presents challenges for parametric SRGMs. Importantly, no single model can accurately predict reliability across different software projects, underscoring the need for careful model selection and expert judgment.

2.3 Non-Parametric Software Reliability Models

Many studies have investigated software bug prediction through the use of ML techniques. For instance, one study introduced a linear auto-regression (AR) method to forecast faulty modules. [89], using historical fault data to forecast future software faults. The AR model was evaluated against the power model (POWM) using root mean square error (RMSE) as the performance metric and tested on three datasets, yielding promising results. Another study explored the effectiveness of different ML methods for fault detection [90], analyzing important prior research for each approach and examining current trends in ML-driven software bug prediction. These studies lay the groundwork for future research in this field. Additionally, a systematic review was carried out on ML-based software bug prediction, encompassing research conducted between 1991 and 2013, analyzed different ML techniques, compared their performance with statistical methods, evaluated strengths and weaknesses, and offered insights for model selection

[91]. A further study provided a benchmark for consistent comparison among bug prediction approaches, presenting a detailed evaluation of well-known methods, introducing a new approach, and assessing its performance using the proposed benchmark [92].

A framework for an object-oriented Software Bug Prediction System was developed by consolidating defect datasets from the PROMISE Software Engineering Repository. [93]. The model was assessed based on accuracy as the performance metric, attaining an average accuracy of 76.27%. Another approach used a genetic algorithm to predict fault-proneness, leveraging count metrics and object-oriented from publicly available software projects [94]. These metrics serve as inputs for the genetic algorithm, which generates rules to classify software modules as defective or non-defective, with the results visualized through a genetic algorithm applet. Additionally, a study assessed different object-oriented metrics through machine learning methods (neural networks and decision trees) and statistical approaches (logical and linear regression) [95]. The findings indicated that Lines of Code (LOC) is moderately effective, Coupling between Objects (CBO) is the most effective metric for class-level bug prediction, and Depth of Inheritance Tree (DIT) along with Number of Children (NOC) are considered unreliable. The study evaluated five widely used ML algorithms for defect prediction—Linear Classifiers (LC), Decision Tree (DT), Artificial Neural Networks (ANNs), Naïve Bayes (NB), and Particle Swarm Optimization (PSO). LC achieved the lowest error rate, followed by DT, while linear classifiers also demonstrated higher overall accuracy compared to the other methods.

The most frequently applied techniques in SDP include DT, BL, ANN, SVM, RBL, and EA. Common metrics in these studies include LOC, object-oriented metrics such as cohesion, coupling, and inheritance, as well as hybrid metrics that combine object-oriented and procedural measures. Most research has utilized datasets from NASA and PROMISE. Various ML techniques and their effectiveness in defect prediction have been discussed, providing guidance for selecting relevant software metrics and appropriate data mining methods to improve software quality [96]. Another study highlighted the most effective metrics for defect prediction [97], including line of code, response for a class, and lack of coding quality.

Popular data mining techniques, including decision trees, C4.5, Naïve Bayes, and k nearest neighbors, have been analyzed to compare their strengths and weaknesses [98]. The findings indicated that factors such as the problem type, dataset, and chosen performance metrics significantly influence each technique's accuracy. Another study examined the correlation between object-oriented metrics and class-level fault proneness [99]. By utilizing ML-based classifiers and statistical approaches, various SDP (SDP) models have been proposed. Multiple classification algorithms including RF, one rule, decision tree, SVM, K star, MLP, KNN, RBF, and NB were applied to forecast software errors across twelve NASA datasets [100], with performance evaluated using AUC, F-measure, recall, accuracy, and precision. Additionally, root cause analysis is used to identify underlying issues for early defect detection. The models also employ clustering techniques, which use unsupervised learning based on data similarities [101], with K means clustering showing the best performance when implemented through the WEKA tool.

ML based classification is also applied for SDP , where various classifiers including decision tree, NB, and ANN were used, yielding promising results [102]. These approaches classify outputs into five categories based on small dataset measurements, with experiments carried out on three publicly available datasets using the WEKA 3.6.9 ML tool. Another study investigated software defect discovery using five classifiers: NB, SVM, KNN, neural networks, and logistic regression [103], employing five NASA metrics datasets, where NB and SVM achieved the best performance on certain datasets. Since software faults greatly affect software quality, removing these faults is crucial to improving overall quality. Various models have been developed to improve software quality by studying the factors that impact software performance and product development [104], integrating size and complexity metrics with models like Bayesian belief networks, genetic algorithms, and neural networks. Another approach focused on efficiently identifying software defects to save time and cost [105], using volume, difficulty, commitment, time estimators, and program length to categorize defects. The study employed the decision tree classifier and ID3 algorithm [106] for defect classification and applied a pattern mining approach to detect faulty patterns, implementing the model in Java.

2.4 Hybrid Model for Software Reliability

This influential study [107] explores the use of NN for forecasting software reliability. The study indicates that neural networks, because of their ability to model complex non-linear relationships, efficiently capture the detailed patterns found in software failure data. The study compares neural network-based predictions with traditional statistical models, showing that NN can provide superior predictive performance due to their adaptability and learning capabilities. Some researchers also present software reliability models that incorporate time-dependent hazard functions. These models consider the evolving nature of software failure processes, where the hazard rate changes over time. The authors present various time-dependent hazard functions and demonstrate their use in predicting software reliability, highlighting the significance of accounting for time-varying factors in reliability modeling. A comprehensive benchmarking framework for evaluating classification models in SDP is also proposed [108], emphasizing the need for standardized evaluation metrics and methodologies to enable fair comparisons across models. Several ML techniques, including DT, SVM, and neural NN, are benchmarked, revealing the strengths and weaknesses of each in predicting software defects. The study indicates that ensemble learning techniques often outperform individual models by combining predictions to enhance accuracy and robustness. Additionally, the use of Bayesian networks for modeling software quality is explored [109]. Bayesian networks provide a probabilistic framework that can incorporate prior knowledge and learn from data, making them suitable for reliability prediction. The authors discuss the construction and parameterization of Bayesian networks for software quality assessment, illustrating how these networks can model dependencies among various software attributes and estimate the probability of defects

The challenge of predicting software quality when only limited project data is available is addressed [110]. The paper explores various machine learning and statistical techniques that can effectively utilize sparse datasets for making reliable predictions. The authors emphasize the significance of feature selection and data preprocessing in enhancing model performance. Their study illustrates that, even with limited data, models like SVM and NN can be fine-tuned to provide accurate software quality predictions. Furthermore, a software reliability growth model that integrates fuzzy parameters has been proposed to handle the inherent uncertainty and imprecision in reliability data. The model is designed to increase the accuracy of reliability predictions by utilizing fuzzy logic to more accurately represent the uncertainties associated with software failures and their detection rates. The authors show that the fuzzy model offers more realistic and flexible predictions compared to traditional crisp models. The paper covers traditional reliability models, such as exponential and Weibull, and introduces advanced techniques including Bayesian methods and neural networks, emphasizing the need to select models based on the software's characteristics and operational environment [111]. A logarithmic Poisson execution time model is proposed for measuring software reliability [112], assuming that failures occur according to a Poisson process and that the failure rate decreases logarithmically over time. The model is mathematically formulated and validated with empirical data, demonstrating its ability to capture the declining failure rate observed in many systems. Additionally, a novel software reliability model incorporating a dynamic fault reduction factor is introduced [113], which accounts for the varying effectiveness of fault detection and correction over time. This factor adjusts failure intensity according to the software's current state, enabling more accurate and responsive reliability predictions. The authors validate their model using real-world software data and show that it outperforms traditional static models.

This study introduces a time-dependent fault detection rate model that reflects the varying rate of fault detection throughout the software lifecycle [114]. This model incorporates a time-varying detection rate function, allowing it to reflect the effects of different testing phases and intensities. The authors outline a complete mathematical framework for the model and demonstrate its application through case studies, highlighting its flexibility and accuracy in predicting software reliability. A hybrid model that enhances neural network predictions with a Kalman filter is proposed [115]. The Kalman filter is employed to iteratively adjust neural network parameters with incoming data, improving both the accuracy and stability of reliability predictions. This approach merges the adaptive learning capabilities of NN with the robustness of Kalman filtering, making it ideal for dynamic and uncertain environments. The authors validate their model's effectiveness through simulation studies. Additionally, an analytical approach for predicting software performance and reliability based on software architecture is presented [116]. The model evaluates the impact of architectural decisions on software reliability by analyzing the interactions between different components and their failure behaviors. The authors create a suite of analytical tools and methods to evaluate the reliability of complex software architectures. and validate their approach through case studies, showing its practical applicability. A neural-fuzzy model that integrates NN and fuzzy logic for predicting software quality is proposed by Lin and Huang. This hybrid model leverages the understanding capabilities of NN and the uncertainty handling of fuzzy logic to provide accurate and interpretable predictions. The authors develop a comprehensive framework for the model and validate it using empirical data, demonstrating its effectiveness in capturing the complex relationships between software metrics and quality attributes.

The use of genetic programming for SRP evolves mathematical expressions and models that best fit the reliability data, providing a flexible and powerful approach to model. The authors demonstrate the application of genetic programming to various reliability datasets, showing that it can produce accurate and robust models that outperform traditional approaches. The application of Hidden Markov Models (HMM) for SRP is explored. HMMs model the state transitions of a software system, providing a dynamic and detailed representation of the failure process. The authors develop an HMM-based reliability model and validate it with empirical data, showing its effectiveness in accurately predicting software reliability and identifying critical states in the software lifecycle. Additionally, a hybrid model combining Support vector regression (SVR) with GA is proposed [117]. GA optimizes the parameters of SVR, enhancing the model's predictive accuracy, while SVR handles nonlinear relationships through robust regression. By combining both techniques, the hybrid approach offers a powerful and flexible framework for reliability prediction. The authors validate their model through empirical studies, showing significant improvements in prediction accuracy over traditional methods. The use of data mining techniques to predict software quality by analyzing process history data is explored [118]. The paper highlights the significance of historical process data in uncovering patterns and trends that can guide quality predictions. By applying various data mining algorithms to process metrics, the authors demonstrate that models based on historical data can effectively predict software defects and quality issues. Their approach underscores the value of leveraging existing data to improve the accuracy of SRPs.

A wavelet neural network (WNN) model for SRP is introduced [119]. The WNN combines wavelet transforms with NN to capture both time-frequency features and nonlinear relationships in the reliability data. Wavelet transforms help in extracting significant features from the data, while NN model the complex interactions between these features. The authors demonstrate that the WNN model achieves higher prediction accuracy than traditional NN and statistical models, making it a valuable tool for software reliability analysis. They also present a comprehensive study comparing various statistical and machine learning methods for software fault prediction [120]. Techniques such as LR, DT, SVM, and NN are evaluated across diverse software project datasets, with the study highlighting the strengths and limitations of each method and offering guidance on their applicability in different contexts. The authors find that ensemble methods, which combine multiple models, often yield the best performance in fault prediction, underscoring the importance of leveraging multiple approaches to improve reliability predictions. An in-depth exploration of logistic regression, a powerful statistical technique used for binary classification problems, including SDP, is provided [121]. The book covers the theoretical foundations of logistic regression, its practical implementation, and various extensions to handle more complex scenarios. The authors discuss model building, variable selection, and model diagnostics, offering a comprehensive guide for practitioners. Logistic regression is highlighted as an effective tool for predicting the presence or absence of software faults based on historical and process data.

A hybrid model combining ANN and regression models to predict software reliability is presented [122], arguing that while traditional statistical models are useful, they struggle with non-linear relationships within software reliability data. The hybrid model combines ANNs, which are adept at capturing complex nonlinear patterns, with regression models that provide interpretability and robustness, thereby leveraging the strengths of both approaches and significantly improving prediction accuracy over standalone ANN or regression models. The study explores the use of fuzzy logic to manage the inherent uncertainty in software reliability data, along with genetic algorithms (GA) for optimizing the prediction model [123]. The fuzzy logic component manages imprecise and uncertain inputs by assigning degrees of truth instead of binary values, enabling more nuanced data interpretation, while the genetic algorithm optimizes model parameters by simulating natural selection. This combined approach improves the model's ability to predict software reliability with greater accuracy and flexibility. Different authors have benchmarked various classification models for SDP, offering a comprehensive framework for performance comparison and highlighting the importance of using multiple metrics and statistical tests to evaluate prediction models. Their findings indicate that ensemble learning techniques, which aggregate predictions from multiple classifiers, generally outperform individual models, demonstrating the potential of ensemble methods to enhance SRPs by leveraging diverse model strengths and mitigating individual weaknesses.

A Bayesian network approach to SDP is introduced [124], leveraging the probabilistic nature of Bayesian networks to model uncertainties and dependencies among software attributes. Bayesian networks offer a structured method to integrate prior knowledge and update predictions as new data becomes available, effectively capturing the complex relationships between software metrics and defect occurrences and providing more accurate and interpretable predictions than traditional statistical models. To enhance software fault prediction, a two-step data preprocessing technique has been proposed, involving feature selection to identify the most relevant software metrics and data transformation to standardize and normalize these features. This approach improves the quality of input data, thereby enhancing the performance, accuracy, and robustness of ML models across diverse datasets. In Esteves et al. [123], research on software development effort estimation integrates fuzzy logic with NN to achieve higher accuracy, where fuzzy logic handles ambiguity in project attributes and NN capture complex non-linear relationships, resulting in a hybrid model that outperforms traditional methods. Additionally, the use of Hidden Markov Models (HMMs) for SRP is explored, modeling probabilistic transitions between software states and demonstrating superior predictive performance compared to static models, particularly in dynamic environments. A hybrid reliability model that incorporates time and fault dependency, using Weibull distributions and machine learning to enhance prediction accuracy in complex software systems, is presented by [125]. Dynamic Bayesian networks (DBNs) for software reliability modeling are explored [126], highlighting their ability to incorporate temporal dynamics and continuously update predictions, thus improving accuracy and adaptability.

The combination of Cox proportional hazards models with ML to predict software defects, leveraging the strengths of both methods to handle time-to-event data and achieve precise predictions, is demonstrated by [127]. Also comparison of various ML techniques for SRP is conducted by this team to finding that DT, SVM, and NN, especially with effective feature selection and preprocessing, significantly enhance prediction accuracy over traditional models. The application of NN in reliability prediction is pioneered by [128], demonstrating their superiority in capturing non-linear relationships and intricate dependencies in software metrics.

Genetic programming (GP) for SRP is explored [129], showcasing its flexibility and robustness in evolving prediction models dynamically. HMMs for reliability prediction are also investigated by [130], emphasizing their effectiveness in modeling stochastic software behavior. The review of ML techniques for fault prediction, highlighting the advantages of ensemble methods and diverse approaches to improve accuracy, is conducted by [131]. The role of data mining in software quality assurance (SQA), which uncovers hidden patterns to predict quality and reliability, is discussed. WNNs for reliability prediction are introduced, combining wavelet transforms with NN to capture time and frequency domain information, thus improving prediction robustness. The study demonstrates the use of NN with object-oriented metrics to predict software quality, highlighting their effectiveness in capturing relationships between metrics and quality attributes. Logistic regression, a robust statistical technique for binary classification tasks such as SDP, is also explored [132], providing a comprehensive guide to its implementation and application in software reliability assessment.

2.5 Optimization Algorithms in Hybrid Models

SRP is essential for estimating the probability that a software system will operate without failure over a specified time period, supporting maintenance planning, risk management, and overall software quality improvement. Optimization algorithms are frequently used to enhance the accuracy and performance of these prediction models. Among them, genetic algorithms (GA), inspired by natural selection, are particularly effective at exploring large solution spaces and fine-tuning model parameters [133]. Particle Swarm Optimization (PSO), simulating social behavior, is adept at fine-tuning model parameters. The effectiveness of a hybrid model combining artificial NN and PSO for improved SRP is demonstrated in [134]. Simulated Annealing (SA) seeks a global optimum by occasionally accepting worse solutions to avoid local minima traps. As shown in [135], SA enhances the global search for optimal solutions in SRP. Ant Colony Optimization (ACO), modeled on the foraging behavior of ants, provides an efficient mechanism for optimizing paths and tuning parameter values. Its adaptive application in SRP demonstrates robust performance in managing dynamic variations and complex operational environments. [136]. DE is known for its simplicity and effectiveness in optimizing continuous variables. A self-adaptive DE algorithm introduced in [137] adjusts control parameters for enhanced numerical optimization, making it suitable for hybrid models in SRP. Cuckoo Search

(CS), leveraging Lévy flight behavior, effectively addresses optimization problems. The authors in [138] explored a CS-based model for SRP, demonstrating its ability to improve prediction accuracy.

Inspired by the foraging behavior of honey bees, the Artificial Bee Colony (ABC) algorithm tackles optimization problems by simulating smart swarm behavior. It is particularly effective for tuning parameters in software reliability models [139]. The Firefly Algorithm (FA), which mimics fireflies' attraction behavior, addresses optimization problems by adjusting light intensity and attraction between fireflies, proving effective in design optimization and stochastic test functions [140]. Harmony Search (HS), inspired by the musical process of creating harmony, mimics musicians' improvisation and has been successfully applied to various optimization problems, including SRP [141]. Inspired by bats' echolocation behavior, the Bat Algorithm (BA) tackles optimization problems by adjusting frequency, loudness, and pulse rates. It is particularly effective for complex software reliability optimization tasks. [142]. Modeled on the social hierarchy and cooperative hunting of grey wolves, the Grey Wolf Optimizer (GWO) addresses optimization problems by efficiently identifying optimal solutions. It is particularly effective for engineering optimization tasks, including software reliability [143]. Inspired by the bubble-net hunting strategy of humpback whales, the Whale Optimization Algorithm (WOA) tackles complex numerical optimization problems by simulating whale foraging. It is particularly valuable for fine-tuning parameters in hybrid software reliability models [144]. Collectively, these algorithms improve the accuracy and reliability of software prediction models, each offering unique strategies to address the challenges of software reliability optimization.

The Jaya algorithm, introduced by R. Venkata Rao [145], is a simple yet powerful optimization algorithm designed to iteratively move towards the optimum while avoiding the worst solutions. Unlike many other algorithms, Jaya is parameter-free, meaning it does not require algorithm- dependent parameters such as crossover or mutation rates, simplifying its application and eliminating the need for parameter tuning. The algorithm initiates by randomly generating a population of candidate solutions and evaluating their fitness. Each candidate solution is then updated based on its proximity to the best and worst solutions in the current population, with the update formula moving the solution towards the best and away from the worst. This approach ensures a global search for the optimum solution. The effectiveness and simplicity of the Jaya algorithm have been demonstrated in various optimization problems, showcasing its potential as a robust tool in the optimization landscape, as highlighted in [146].

2.6 Research Gaps

After reviewing numerous papers related to SRP models, defect prediction models, and fault prediction models, we identified several research gaps, which are described below.

- Various parametric SRM have been widely used in the literature. These models are built with numerous constraints and are effective when the data is simple, well-structured, and follows predictable patterns. However, in real-world software defects, the data is often chaotic, noisy, and complex, which limits the effectiveness of parametric models. The unpredictable nature of real-world defects makes it challenging for traditional models to accurately capture the complex behaviors and relationships within the data, thereby reducing their reliability and performance in practical applications.
- To manage the chaotic nature of software defect data, machine learning models have shown markedly better performance than traditional software reliability models. Techniques such as SVM, ELM, and DT effectively capture the complex patterns and relationships inherent in software defect data. By utilizing advanced algorithms and computational resources, these machine learning approaches can handle large, noisy datasets and deliver more accurate SRPs, making them essential tools for improving the prediction and management of software defects.
- Studies from various domains indicate that optimization algorithms are highly effective for feature selection in machine learning models. These techniques help eliminate irrelevant or redundant features, enabling the model to concentrate on the most important variables. Models that integrate optimization-based feature selection have been shown to achieve higher accuracy and efficiency by refining the input data. This process not only simplifies the model and reduces overfitting but also enhances the overall reliability and robustness of SRPs.
- The problem of class imbalance, frequently observed in software reliability datasets, can be effectively mitigated using over-sampling and under-sampling methods that rebalance the dataset and enhance prediction accuracy. These approaches modify class distributions

to prevent models from favouring the majority class, thereby improving their ability to detect defects. Furthermore, optimization algorithms can complement these techniques by selecting the most informative features and fine-tuning model parameters to better manage imbalance, resulting in more precise and dependable software defect and reliability predictions.

- Software defect data is inherently complex and often exhibits chaotic, non-linear behavior that traditional modeling techniques struggle to represent accurately. To address these challenges, a hybrid modeling approach that integrates parametric (traditional) models with non-parametric machine learning methods is proposed. This combination harnesses the strengths of both approaches—merging the structured, rule-based characteristics of parametric models with the flexibility and learning capability of machine learning techniques. As a result, the hybrid model can more effectively capture the unpredictable and dynamic nature of software defects, leading to enhanced prediction accuracy and greater reliability in software systems.
- Although Reinforcement learning has achieved notable success across various domains, its application in SDP remains largely unexplored. This gap offers a promising direction for future research to examine how reinforcement learning can be leveraged in this area. By utilizing its ability to learn optimal strategies through continuous interaction and feedback, reinforcement learning could greatly enhance SDP models. Such an approach would enable models to adapt dynamically to changing data and evolving software environments, thereby improving prediction accuracy, defect detection, and overall software reliability.

To address the identified research gaps, this thesis adopts a structured chapter-wise approach. The limitations of traditional parametric reliability models and the need for robust machine learning based prediction are addressed in Chapter 3, which proposes a novel hybrid Jaya Optimization and Extreme Learning Machine model to improve prediction accuracy on complex and noisy datasets. The challenges related to feature redundancy, high dimensionality, and class imbalance are addressed in Chapter 4, where Jaya Optimization is integrated with ensemble learning and SMOTE to enhance reliability prediction performance. The need for hybrid modeling to capture both nonlinear learning behavior and temporal characteristics of software reliability data is addressed in Chapter 5, which presents an optimized ANN–SARIMA framework enhanced by Jaya Optimization. Together, these chapters systematically address the major research gaps identified in the literature and contribute to the advancement of effective and reliable software reliability prediction models.

CHAPTER:3 A Novel Hybrid JAYA Optimization Algorithm and Extreme Learning Machine Classifier (JAYA-ELM) for Software reliability prediction

3.1 Introduction

SRP aims to estimate the likelihood that a software system or application will operate without errors over a specific period or under particular conditions. This process involves using various quantitative and qualitative methodologies to forecast software reliability before deployment in real-world scenarios. The goal is to identify potential issues and allocate resources more effectively to enhance the software product's dependability. Methods for predicting software reliability are broadly categorized into two groups. The first group includes non-parametric methods, which use observable failure data without assuming a specific probability distribution or complexity in software defect data points. Major non-parametric techniques include the Mean Cumulative function (MCF) and the Empirical Reliability Growth (ERG) model [147]. The second group consists of parametric methods, which assume a predefined probability distribution for software failures based on historical data and estimate the parameters of that distribution to predict software defects. Common parametric models include the Exponential, Weibull, and Lognormal distribution models [148]. The SRP process typically involves several sequential steps. It begins with data collection, followed by meticulous data analysis. A suitable model is then selected, and parameters are estimated to facilitate reliability estimation. The results are interpreted to inform decision-making. It is essential to recognize that SRP is not an exact science. The accuracy of any predictive model largely depends on the quality and relevance of historical failure data, as well as the suitability of the selected prediction approach. Despite these limitations, such forecasts offer valuable insights that can guide software development and maintenance efforts, helping to minimize failures and enhance overall software performance and quality.

SRP offers several benefits in software development and maintenance, including early identification of potential risks, optimization of resource allocation, improved testing mechanisms and strategies, enhanced decision-making, risk assessment, improved customer experience, cost savings, quality improvement, and early issue detection. While numerous traditional models exist for SRP, machine learning (ML) techniques offer additional benefits and improved performance that traditional models do not provide. ML approaches are utilized in SRP for several reasons. Firstly, ML models can capture complex and non-linear correlations between various software indicators and identify patterns in data that traditional statistical models may not handle effectively. Secondly, ML approaches facilitate optimal feature selection by automatically selecting or extracting relevant features from a large pool of software measurements, thereby reducing dimensionality and focusing on the most impactful elements influencing reliability, which improves prediction performance. Thirdly, ML approaches such as ensemble methods [149] and Deep Learning can effectively manage high-dimensional data, extracting significant information during model training and tuning. Additionally, ML strategies such as oversampling, undersampling, and cost-sensitive learning can effectively handle imbalanced datasets, where non-failure instances vastly outnumber failure instances [150]. This versatility allows ML models to adapt to changes in software development practices, technology stacks, or project characteristics. On-parametric ML approaches can manage various data types, including categorical, numerical and textual data. This adaptability enables SRP models to incorporate multiple information sources and extract relevant insights. ML-based prediction models have the potential to achieve improved accuracy, uncover hidden patterns, and provide more comprehensive insights into the factors driving software reliability [151]. Commonly used ML algorithms for SRP include RF, which employs multiple decision trees to enhance robustness and reduce overfitting, and SVMs [152], which perform well in high-dimensional spaces, especially when the number of features exceeds the number of samples. ANNs, inspired by the human brain, effectively capture complex patterns and can be further improved using advanced architectures such as CNNs and RNNs [153]. Other algorithms like Naive Bayes and KNN also offer strong classification capabilities. The choice of algorithm should depend on the specific problem and dataset [154].

The main objective is to estimate and evaluate the reliability of software systems before their deployment or release. By proactively assessing software reliability, developers and project managers can gain valuable insights into potential risks and challenges that may arise during the software's operational lifespan, allowing them to address and mitigate the risk of software failure. This paper presents a comprehensive framework aimed at anticipating software issues by integrating the ELM with the Jaya optimization algorithm (JAYA-ELM).The proposed hybrid JAYA-ELM model introduces a novel approach to SRP by combining the strengths of the JAYA optimization algorithm and the ELM. This work offers several key contributions and innovations: The JAYA algorithm simplifies the optimization process by eliminating the need for algorithm-specific parameters, making the model easier to implement and more scalable compared to traditional methods. Additionally, JAYA's ability to consistently find global optima ensures that the model effectively navigates complex high-dimensional problems, avoiding local minima that often hinder other approaches. The ELM component contributes by providing rapid training speeds and excellent generalization performance, enabling the hybrid model to efficiently handle large datasets while maintaining high prediction accuracy. Furthermore, the hybrid JAYA-ELM model is designed to minimize the risk of overfitting and is adaptable across various SRP tasks, making it more robust and reliable than existing techniques. Finally, this model addresses critical gaps in the current literature by providing a more accurate, efficient, and reliable framework for SRP, significantly advancing the state of the art in this field. Our model's efficacy has been rigorously assessed through validation against 20 distinct publicly available software defect datasets. The experimental findings conclusively demonstrate that our hybrid JAYA-ELM model surpasses benchmark models in predictive performance.

3.2 Proposed (JAYA-ELM) Model

Effective feature selection plays a critical role in improving the performance and efficiency of machine learning models, particularly in software reliability prediction tasks. In this study, the complete dataset containing all available features is processed using the Jaya Optimization algorithm to identify the most significant attributes. This optimization process focuses on selecting relevant features that contribute meaningfully to prediction accuracy while eliminating redundant and irrelevant information. As a result, an optimal feature set is obtained and refined for subsequent machine learning training. This refinement minimizes noise during the learning process and enhances computational efficiency. The optimized dataset is then employed for classification using the ELM, which is well suited for binary classification problems due to its fast learning capability and strong generalization performance. The overall workflow, illustrated in Fig. 3.1, highlights the crucial role of feature selection in strengthening the effectiveness of the proposed JAYA-ELM architecture.

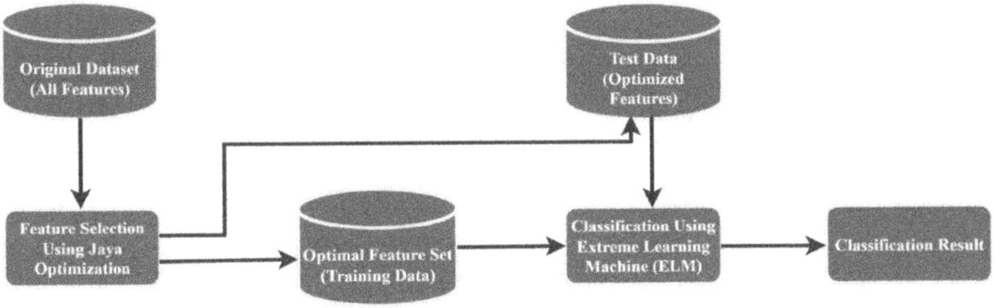

Fig. 3.1 Architecture of Proposed JAYA-ELM Model

The feature selection process is designed to identify the most informative attributes while reducing redundancy and improving classification efficiency. In the proposed framework, input features F1 to F40 are represented in binary form across multiple instances A1 to A50, where values of 0 and 1 indicate the absence or presence of specific characteristics. During optimization, multiple candidate feature subsets are generated and evaluated through the Extreme Learning Machine classifier. The ELM, which is a single hidden layer feedforward neural network with randomly assigned and fixed input weights, enables fast learning and strong generalization capability. For each candidate solution, the ELM produces a fitness score expressed as a percentage, reflecting the classification performance achieved using the selected features. These fitness values act as the guiding criterion for the JAYA optimization process, which iteratively updates solutions by moving toward the best performing feature set while avoiding the least effective ones. This iterative evaluation and refinement mechanism ensures the selection of a compact and relevant feature subset that enhances prediction accuracy and reduces computational overhead. Additionally, the integration of feature selection with classification allows a direct assessment of feature relevance based on model performance rather than statistical assumptions alone. As a result, the proposed framework improves the robustness and reliability of the learning process. Figure 3.2 illustrates the proposed feature selection framework based on the JAYA optimization algorithm integrated with the ELM classifier.

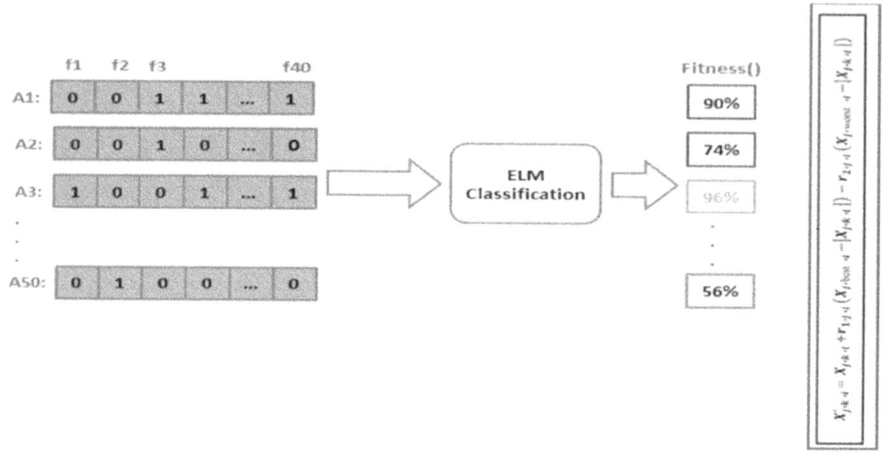

Fig. 3.2 Proposed feature selection techniques

3.3 Experimental Setup

This study introduces an innovative method that builds upon the concepts discussed in paper [156]. To verify the theoretical framework developed in this study, experiments were conducted in a Python environment. The results of these experiments were assessed using performance metrics to evaluate the effectiveness and robustness of the proposed software fault or reliability prediction model. As described in the previous section, two datasets were employed for this study: the NASA MDP dataset and a Java open-source projects dataset. Prior to model implementation, several preprocessing steps were performed, including data normalization, handling of multi-label classes, and treatment of missing values. The Jaya-ELM model incorporates the Jaya optimization algorithm to fine-tune the ELM parameters, thereby enhancing the accuracy of SRP. Define a cost function f (θ) based on prediction error or loss (e.g., Mean Squared Error, Cross-Entropy Loss):

$$f(\theta) = Loss(T, H\beta) \tag{3.1}$$

Initialize $\theta = \{W, b\} for\ ELM$

Use the JAYA algorithm to minimize the cost function: $\min_{\theta} f(\theta)$

After optimization, use the final optimized parameters $\theta^* = \{W^*, b^*\}$ to calculate the ELM output H^* and thr output weights β^* :

$$\beta^* = (H^*)^{\dagger}T \tag{3.2}$$

The predicted software reliability $\hat{T}$ is then given by $\hat{T} = H^* \beta^*$

The overall equation for the JAYA-ELM model can be summarized as:

$$\hat{T} = g(XW^* + b^*)\beta^* \tag{3.3}$$

Where W^* and b^* are the optimized parameters obtained through the JAYA algorithm.

This hybrid approach leverages the optimization power of the JAYA algorithm to fine-tune the ELM parameters, resulting in a model that is more accurate for SRP.

3.3.1 Experimental Configuration

This model simulated with Python 3.11 with different packages such as Matplotlib, Pandas, Numpy, and Seaborn on Windows 10 operating system with Intel Core i5-10400U- CPU @2.90GHz processor and 16 GB RAM.

3.3.2 Parameter Description

The parameters used in our experimental setup for ELM and Jaya algorithm are mentioned below in Table 3.1.

Table 3.1 Experimental parameters of JAYA-ELM hybrid Model

Parameter	Details
Extreme Learning Machine (ELM)	
Activation function	Radial Basis function (RBF)
Cross Validation (N)	10
Hidden Weight Distribution	(-1, 1)
Bias Distribution	(0, 1)
Data Train: Test Ratio	70:30
Data Normalization	Min-Max
Jaya Optimization Algorithm	
Maximum Iteration	100
Number of Agent (Initial)	50

3.3.3 Performance Evaluation

The performance metrics of our proposed hybrid model are based on four key cases: True Positive (TP), True Negative (TN), False Positive (FP), and False Negative (FN). Total positive instances are represented by P, while total negative instances are denoted as N. TP signifies the correct classification of a positive instance, indicating accurate identification of the desired outcome. Conversely, FN denotes the misclassification of a positive instance as negative, indicating a failure to identify it. TN represents the accurate classification of a negative instance, affirming correct absence recognition. Finally, FP occurs when a negative instance is incorrectly labeled as positive, suggesting an erroneous indication of presence These distinctions play a vital role in assessing the effectiveness and reliability of classification models and diagnostic tests, providing valuable insights into their performance and areas for potential enhancement. In the context of software fault prediction (SFP), the positive class represents defective modules. In this study, multiple performance metrics were employed to evaluate the effectiveness of the proposed model and to compare its performance with existing models reported in the literature. Among these metrics, accuracy plays a crucial role as it represents the proportion of correctly classified instances among the total number of samples. It reflects the model's overall capability to correctly predict both positive and negative cases. Since software reliability prediction requires dependable and consistent classification outcomes, accuracy provides an essential measure of how well the proposed model performs across the entire dataset, thereby justifying its use as a primary evaluation metric.

$$Accuracy = TP + TN/(P + N) \tag{3.4}$$

3.3.4 Data on Software Measurement

We validated the proposed model using software defect datasets obtained from the PROMISE repository and compared its performance with existing ML models reported in the literature [155]. The descriptive statistics of all datasets used in this study are presented in Tables 3.2 and 3.3.

Table 3.2 Nasa datasets description

Input dataset	No. of Samples	No. of features	No. of True Values	No. of false Values	Ratio of false cases	Description
MW1	403	38	372	31	8%	A "C"-coded zero-gravity combustion experiment.
PC1	1109	22	1032	77	7%	C-coded flight software for an earth-orbiting spacecraft.
PC3	1563	38	1403	160	10%	C-coded flight software for an Earth-orbiting spacecraft.
PC4	1458	38	1280	178	12%	"C"-coded flight software for an Earth-orbiting spacecraft.
JM1	10885	22	8779	2106	19%	JM1: a real-time predictive ground system, built in "C".
KC1	2109	22	326	1783	85%	"C++" storage management for ground data reception and processing.
KC2	522	22	107	415	80%	Ground data reception and processing storage managed in "C++".
CM1	344	39	42	302	88%	Spacecraft instrument written in C
PC5	17001	40	503	16498	97%	Cockpit security increase system written in C++

Table 3.3 Java datasets description

Input dataset	No. of Samples	No. of features	No. of True Values	No. of false Values	Ratio of false cases	Description
Ant1.6	351	21	259	92	26%	Ant offers built-in tasks for compiling, assembling, testing, and running Java applications.
Camel1.4	872	21	727	145	17%	Camel enables defining routing and mediation rules in domain-specific languages.
Ivy 1.4	241	21	225	16	7%	Apache Ivy™: a potent Java™ dependency manager.
Ivy 2	352	21	312	40	11%	Apache Ivy™: powerful Java™ dependency manager.
Jedit4.1	312	21	233	79	25%	JUnit: test framework using annotations to specify test methods.
log4j1.1	109	21	72	37	34%	Log4j 2 allows users to define their own log levels.
Lucene2.2	247	21	103	144	58%	Apache Lucene™: high-performance search engine library in Java.
poi2.5	385	21	137	248	64%	Apache Lucene™: high-performance search engine in Java.
poi3.0	442	21	161	281	64%	Apache Lucene™: high-performance Java search engine.
Synapse1.2	256	21	170	86	34%	Synapse excels in XML, Web Services, and REST support.

3.4 Algorithmic Flow of the Proposed JAYA–ELM Based Feature Selection Model

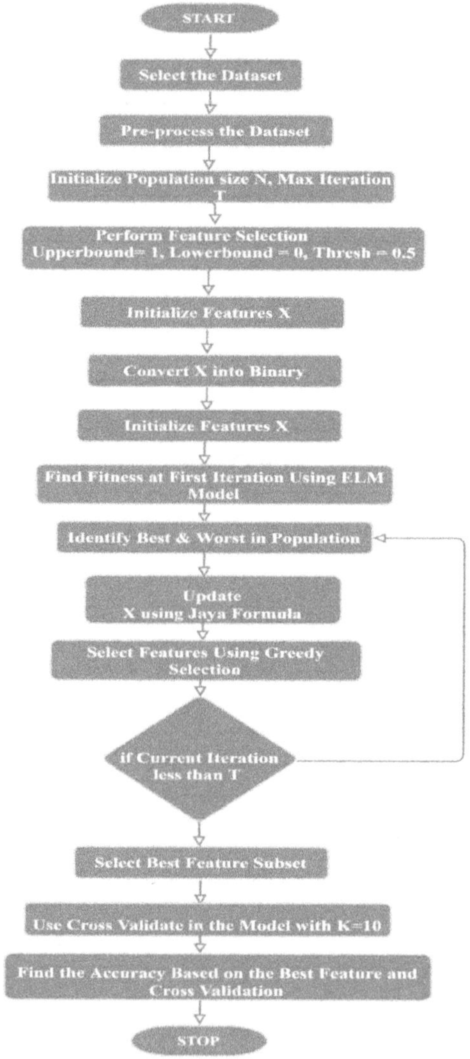

Fig. 3.3 Proposed JAYA-ELM hybrid model

To systematically improve model performance through feature selection and evaluation with an ELM model, follow this approach. The process starts by selecting an appropriate dataset and preprocessing it to handle categorical variables, missing values, and scaling of numerical features. Model parameters, including the maximum number of iterations (T) and population size (N), are then set, along with upper and lower bounds and a feature selection threshold, and the feature set (X) is converted into a binary format. In the initial iteration, the fitness of each individual is evaluated using the ELM model, the best and worst solutions are identified, and features are updated according to the Jaya optimization formula. Greedy feature selection is applied iteratively until the maximum number of iterations is reached, after which the optimal feature subset is determined. The predictive accuracy of the selected features is then assessed using K-fold cross-validation, typically with K=10. This structured approach provides a clear and effective method for identifying relevant features and enhancing model performance.

3.5 Result Analysis

To evaluate the performance of our models, we conducted two separate experiments. The first focused on measuring accuracy using ELM classification, while the second experiment combined the JAYA algorithm with ELM to optimize feature selection. In this second experiment, both the processing time and predictive accuracy were assessed. We also compared the training durations of the two experiments to understand differences in efficiency. Accuracy was analyzed by considering the minimum, average, and maximum values obtained. To ensure the reliability of the results, 10-fold cross validation was applied. Additionally, the ELM model was tested with varying numbers of hidden neurons, including 10, 25, 50, and 100, to examine their impact on overall performance.

3.5.1 Result Analysis of Promise Repository (NASA)

In this section, we present a detailed analysis of the PC5 dataset from the Promise repository, which includes 17,000 samples and 40 features. We employed the ELM with varying numbers of hidden neurons on this dataset, resulting in different outcomes. Using 10 hidden neurons, we achieved accuracies ranging from 0.967 to 0.977, with a training time of 0.0312 seconds. Increasing the number of hidden neurons to 25 resulted in accuracies from 0.96 to 0.983 and a training time of 0.0696 seconds. With 50 hidden neurons, the accuracies ranged from 0.963 to

0.98, and the training time increased to 0.1575 seconds. Finally, with 100 hidden neurons, the accuracies ranged from 0.963 to 0.978, with a training time of 0.3470 seconds. These results highlight that increasing the number of hidden neurons extends the training duration, potentially leading to improved accuracy. Additionally, employing optimization algorithms might further enhance accuracy beyond the reported results.

Using our proposed hybrid algorithm, Jaya-ELM, the Jaya algorithm selected 4 optimal features for both 10 and 25 hidden neurons. With 10 hidden neurons, accuracies ranged from 0.963 to 0.977, achieved in a training time of 0.0310 seconds. With 25 hidden neurons, accuracies ranged from 0.961 to 0.983, with a training time of 0.0644 seconds. For 50 hidden neurons, the algorithm selected 6 optimal features, resulting in accuracies ranging from 0.965 to 0.981, with a training time of 0.1249 seconds. Finally, with 100 hidden neurons, 4 features were selected, and accuracies ranged from 0.962 to 0.982, with a training time of 0.2811 seconds. Notably, our proposed ELM-JAYA model reduced training time compared to ELM while demonstrating overall accuracy improvements. These findings were consistent across the remaining nine datasets from the Promise repository, where the proposed model also achieved enhanced accuracy and reduced training time compared to ELM. Further details and analysis are provided in Table 4.

Table 3.4 Result analysis of ELM-JAYA hybrid model on Promise repository (NASA)

Dataset Name	Number of Hidden Neuron in ELM	No. of feature selected in ELM+JAYA	Time taken for feature selection	Training time (ELM) in second	Training time (ELM + Jaya) in second	10 fold Cross Validation (ELM) Accuracy			10 fold Cross Validation (ELM + JAYA) Accuracy (Our Proposed Model)		
						Min	Mean	Max	Min	Mean	Max
Cm1	10	11	15.7173	0.0149	0.0039	0.75	0.875	0.958	0.828	0.896	1
	25	20	21.1048	0.0468	0.00499	0.708	0.879	0.958	0.771	0.888	1
	50	16	30.0648	0.2423	0.0069	0.75	0.846	0.958	0.8	0.885	0.971
	100	20	50.0451	0.0413	0.0119	0.708	0.8	0.875	0.743	0.86	0.941
Jm1	10	4	86.3536	0.0199	0.002	0.779	0.806	0.826	0.798	0.812	0.829
	25	4	225.4398	0.04288	0.0378	0.79	0.811	0.83	0.78	0.813	0.84
	50	5	472.4373	0.1156	0.0677	0.798	0.811	0.83	0.796	0.815	0.84
	100	3	1052.3193	0.2013	0.2962	0.794	0.81	0.824	0.799	0.813	0.84
Kc1	10	6	24.4926	0.002	0.001	0.823	0.851	0.899	0.804	0.857	0.939
	25	9	42.972	0.0071	0.0155	0.817	0.857	0.892	0.79	0.852	0.899
	50	7	87.0519	0.0139	0.0156	0.817	0.854	0.884	0.817	0.864	0.911
	100	6	259.9243	0.0398	0.0408	0.809	0.849	0.892	0.824	0.86	0.892
Kc2	10	9	15.924	0.007	0.0156	0.73	0.819	0.917	0.784	0.835	0.892
	25	3	15.5943	0.0063	0.0024	0.722	0.846	0.8	0.643	0.824	1

	50	7	30.6082	0.0049	0.0156	0.676	0.8116	0.889	0.5	0.819	1
	100	4	52.5341	0.0089	0.0156	0.639	0.791	0.861	0.571	0.809	1
Mw1	10	12	17.2016	0.0029	0.0049	0.786	0.918	1	0.786	0.925	1
	25	4	21.9304	0.0083	0.0059	0.857	0.925	0.964	0.857	0.918	0.964
	50	8	31.4156	0.0055	0.0079	0.821	0.894	0.964	0.857	0.915	0.964
	100	19	56.452	0.0089	0.0129	0.75	0.869	0.964	0.714	0.875	0.965
Pc1	10	3	20.0264	0.0049	0.0027	0.897	0.929	0.961	0.897	0.933	0.974
	25	4	30.8951	0.0039	0.0023	0.897	0.928	0.961	0.87	0.937	0.974
	50	6	50.8699	0.0108	0.0156	0.872	0.924	0.974	0.883	0.924	0.974
	100	7	108.3259	0.0259	0.0312	0.831	0.903	0.949	0.82	0.914	0.961
Pc3	10	5	23.411	0.0029	0.0049	0.862	0.897	0.927	0.844	0.897	0.945
	25	12	38.2535	0.0079	0.0156	0.844	0.892	0.918	0.853	0.897	0.927
	50	18	75.7887	0.0129	0.0156	0.864	0.891	0.936	0.845	0.895	0.934
	100	11	153.535	0.0319	0.0319	0.862	0.887	0.936	0.826	0.887	0.954
Pc4	10	6	24.0369	0.011	0.0069	0.823	0.876	0.912	0.794	0.877	0.921
	25	8	37.3229	0.012	0.0099	0.863	0.904	0.921	0.892	0.904	0.941
	50	12	82.3896	0.013	0.0103	0.843	0.902	0.951	0.843	0.906	0.961
	100	17	148.8763	0.0309	0.0156	0.823	0.895	0.941	0.872	0.902	0.941
Pc5	10	4	117.08344	0.0312	0.0310	0.967	0.972	0.977	0.963	0.973	0.979
	25	4	339.9454	0.0696	0.0644	0.960	0.971	0.983	0.961	0.973	0.983
	50	6	704.4899	0.1575	0.1249	0.963	0.972	0.98	0.965	0.973	0.981
	100	4	1428.2383	0.3470	0.2811	0.963	0.973	0.978	0.962	0.973	0.982

3.5.2 Result Analysis of Promise Repository (JAVA)

We examined the Camel 1.4 dataset from the Java repository, which consists of 872 samples and 21 features. ELM was applied with varying numbers of hidden neurons, yielding notable results. With 10 hidden neurons, the ELM achieved accuracies ranging from 0.738 to 0.902, with a training time of 0.0169 seconds. Increasing to 25 hidden neurons improved accuracies to between 0.754 and 0.918 and reduced the training time to 0.0084 seconds. Using 50 hidden neurons resulted in accuracies ranging from 0.738 to 0.885, with a training time of 0.0095 seconds. With 100 hidden neurons, accuracies varied from 0.705 to 0.885, and the training time increased to 0.0207 seconds.

Subsequently, the Jaya-ELM algorithm was applied to the same dataset. With 10 hidden neurons, the algorithm selected 7 optimal features and achieved accuracies between 0.77 and 0.95, with a reduced training time of 0.0032 seconds. Increasing to 25 hidden neurons led to the selection of 8 optimal features, with accuracies ranging from 0.77 to 0.885 and a training time of 0.0049 seconds. For 50 hidden neurons, 6 optimal features were chosen, achieving accuracies from 0.787 to 0.885, and a training time of 0.0052 seconds. Finally, with 100 hidden neurons, 11 features were selected, resulting in accuracies from 0.754 to 0.902, with a training time of 0.0062 seconds. The ELM-JAYA model demonstrated significant improvements over the standard ELM, showing reduced training times and enhanced accuracy across different configurations. These benefits were consistently observed in the other nine datasets from the Java repository, highlighting the effectiveness of the proposed model.

Table 3.5 Result analysis of ELM-JAYA hybrid model on Promise repository (JAVA)

Dataset Name	Number of Hidden Neuron in ELM	No. of feature selected in ELM+JAYA	Time taken for feature selection	Training time (ELM) in second	Training time (ELM + Jaya) in second	10 fold Cross Validation (ELM) Accuracy			10 fold Cross Validation (ELM + JAYA) Accuracy (Our Proposed Model)		
						Min	Mean	Max	Min	Mean	Max
Ant1.6	10	5	18.341	0.0156	0.013	0.64	0.775	0.88	0.64	0.777	0.96
	25	11	23.4673	0.0134	0.0051	0.667	0.759	0.84	0.667	0.8	0.917
	50	8	32.6953	0.0209	0.0089	0.64	0.78	0.88	0.667	0.784	0.92
	100	6	55.7452	0.0319	55.74	0.583	0.717	0.833	0.625	0.735	0.92
Camel1.4	10	7	21.9828	0.0169	0.0032	0.738	0.828	0.902	0.77	0.831	0.95
	25	8	31.8962	0.0084	0.0049	0.754	0.838	0.918	0.77	0.843	0.951
	50	9	47.1527	0.0095	0.0052	0.738	0.81	0.885	0.787	0.838	0.885
	100	11	92.9492	0.0207	0.0062	0.705	0.826	0.885	0.754	0.831	0.902
Ivy 1.4	10	2	13.2921	0.0167	0.0079	0.823	0.929	1	0.823	0.94	1
	25	10	16.9356	0.0039	0.0039	0.823	0.916	1	0.823	0.929	1
	50	8	24.3411	0.0039	0.0039	0.706	0.881	0.941	0.882	0.923	1
	100	8	47.8572	0.0059	0.0069	0.706	0.822	0.941	0.75	0.857	1
Ivy 2	10	5	15.8137	0.0049	0.0039	0.75	0.894	1	0.8	0.894	1

	25	8	16.9974	0.0049	0.0099	0.792	0.898	0.96	0.8	0.899	1
	50	10	25.1443	0.0049	0.0164	0.792	0.882	0.96	0.8	0.882	1
	100	10	44.9003	0.0169	0.0149	0.72	0.814	0.92	0.75	0.829	0.958
Jedit4.1	10	7	15.1984	0.0062	0.0059	0.636	0.78	0.909	0.714	0.802	0.909
	25	7	18.5323	0.0079	0.0156	0.591	0.771	0.905	0.727	0.821	0.909
	50	12	26.665	0.0079	0.0156	0.667	0.811	0.954	0.714	0.82	0.909
	100	8	43.7738	0.0079	0.0156	0.636	0.739	0.818	0.636	0.803	0.909
log4j1.1	10	6	14.0442	0.0049	0.0049	0.571	0.761	1	0.625	0.778	1
	25	6	15.8784	0.0049	0.0049	0.375	0.741	1	0.428	0.775	1
	50	9	19.5017	0.0094	0.0049	0.25	0.618	1	0.428	0.668	1
	100	10	34.1703	0.0094	0.0069	0.286	0.484	0.625	0.375	0.578	0.875
Lucene2.2	10	7	14.313	0.0039	0.0069	0.412	0.581	0.722	0.47	0.639	0.765
	25	10	16.9536	0.0039	0.0069	0.294	0.599	0.764	0.47	0.634	0.765
	50	6	23.02469	0.0039	0.0069	0.47	0.547	0.706	0.389	0.565	0.706
	100	5	41.1665	0.0039	0.0069	0.353	0.494	0.647	0.353	0.553	0.647
Poi2.5	10	5	15.8611	0.0039	0.0059	0.63	0.762	0.852	0.555	0.78	0.889
	25	6	19.4664	0.0039	0.0156	0.63	0.765	0.889	0.667	0.781	0.889
	50	8	28.3843	0.0049	0.0156	0.667	0.755	0.852	0.667	0.814	0.926
	100	7	47.2949	0.0156	0.0156	0.63	0.728	0.851	0.667	0.758	0.889
Poi3.0	10	9	15.4711	0.0039	0.0069	0.516	0.699	0.806	0.581	0.748	0.9
	25	10	21.4941	0.0039	0.0069	0.581	0.732	0.833	0.633	0.763	0.903

	50	2	29.8167	0.0059	0.0069	0.484	0.719	0.839	0.613	0.728	0.871
	100	8	52.20189	0.0156	0.0156	0.433	0.653	0.774	0.581	0.741	0.903
Synapse1.2	10	5	14.687	0.0029	0.0156	0.444	0.725	0.889	0.556	0.715	0.944
	25	6	18.649	0.0029	0.0156	0.555	0.738	0.889	0.611	0.715	0.833
	50	12	25.4355	0.0059	0.0156	0.5	0.653	0.778	0.611	0.726	0.889
	100	8	41.7477	0.0156	0.0156	0.5	0.598	0.722	0.5	0.687	0.944
Xerces1.3	10	5	19.903	0.0152	0.0054	0.75	0.839	0.937	0.75	0.865	0.937
	25	6	25.5471	0.0156	0.0124	0.774	0.842	0.906	0.742	0.855	0.935
	50	10	35.9973	0.0049	0.0089	0.742	0.852	0.969	0.781	0.876	1
	100	9	60.5102	0.01562	0.021	0.71	0.861	0.969	0.774	0.867	1

3.5.3 Comparison of Results

In the results comparison section of our study, detailed in Sections 3.5.1 and 3.5.2, we elucidate the comparative performance of our proposed hybrid JAYA-ELM model against established methodologies in SRP. Our analysis reveals a substantial reduction in training time when employing feature selection via the Jaya algorithm, resulting in expedited model training compared to the feature-unselected ELM counterpart. This efficiency enhancement is consistently observed across both the Java and PROMISE datasets, validating the efficacy of our feature selection approach.

Our comparative analysis against existing literature highlights the superior predictive capability of our JAYA-ELM model compared to alternative methodologies such as ELM-FA, ELM-GA, ELM-PSO, ELM-BESTF, and ELM-GREDDY. For example, in the KC2 dataset from the NASA repository, where other models achieved accuracies between 0.794 and 0.806, our JAYA-ELM model attained a notably higher accuracy of 0.835, indicating a significant performance enhancement. This trend of improved predictive accuracy was consistently observed across datasets like PC1, PC3, PC4, and PC5, reinforcing the strength and adaptability of our approach across varied data scenarios. Similarly, in our comparison with methods like GA-SVM, PSO-SVM, SVM, WASVM, and GAWhale-SVM, our JAYA-ELM model consistently outperformed them. For instance, in the MW1 dataset, our model achieved an accuracy of 0.925, surpassing the range of 0.917 to 0.923 achieved by other models.

We also compared the performance of our JAYA-ELM model with various alternative methods like GA-SVM, PSO-SVM, SVM, WASVM, and GAWhale-SVM [157]. Our model consistently demonstrated superior predictive capabilities. In the MW1 dataset, our JAYA-ELM model achieved an accuracy of 0.925, surpassing the accuracies of 0.917 to 0.923 achieved by other models. This trend of improved accuracy was also evident in the KC1 and KC2 datasets, underscoring the robustness and adaptability of our approach. Similarly, in the Ivy-1.4 dataset from the Java repository, our model outperformed others with an accuracy of 0.94, compared to accuracies ranging from 0.925 to 0.933 in competing models. This pattern of enhanced accuracy was consistently replicated across multiple datasets, including Camel-1.4, Ivy-2, Jedit-4.1, Lucene2.2, Synapse1.2, and Xerces1. Figure 3.4 depicts the comparison results using 10 hidden neurons of our model with ELM-FA, ELM-GA, PSO, BESTF, and GREDDY [158]. These comparative findings underscore the practical utility of integrating Jaya optimization with ELM for SRP, highlighting the efficacy of feature selection techniques in enhancing predictive performance. Our research contributes methodological insights to the field, offering practitioners a refined framework for accurate and efficient software reliability estimation. Future endeavors may focus on further optimization strategies and model refinement to address evolving software engineering challenges comprehensively.

Table 3.6 Comparison results of ELM-JAYA hybrid model

	(Arora et al. 2019)[155]					(Alsghaier et al. 2020)[157]			(Alsghaier et al. 2021)[158]		Our Proposed Model (JAYA-ELM)	
	ELM-fA	**ELM-GA**	**ELM-PSO**	**ELM-BESTF**	**ELM-GREEDY**	**GA-SVM**	**PSO-SVM**	**GAPSO-SVM**	**WA-SVM**	**GAWhale-SVM**	**ELM**	**ELM-JAYA**
						Promise Nasa Datasets						
CM1	-	-	-	-	-	0.903	0.903	0.904	0.901	0.905	0.875	0.896
JM1	-	-	-	-	-	-	-	-	-	-	0.806	0.812
KC1	-	-	-	-	-	0.851	0.851	0.843	0.845	0.842	0.851	0.857
KC2	0.802	0.806	0.799	0.794	0.804	0.798	0.783	0.806	0.816	0.800	0.819	0.835
MW1	-	-	-	-	-	0.918	0.917	0.915	0.923	0.918	0.918	0.925
PC1	0.927	0.923	0.929	0.924	0.923	0.936	0.936	0.938	0.934	0.936	0.929	0.933
PC3	0.87	0.868	0.868	0.872	0.87	0.901	0.902	0.904	0.900	0.902	0.897	0.897
PC4	0.891	0.892	0.889	0.893	0.893	0.882	0.879	0.877	0	0	0.876	0.877
PC5	0.971	0.973	0.971	0.97	0.971	-	-	-	-	-	0.972	0.973
						Java Datasets						
Ant-1.6	-	-	-	-	-	0.783	0.771	0.811	0.783	0.794	0.775	0.777
Camel-1.4		-	-	-	-	0.831	0.821	0.831	0.826	0.827	0.828	0.831
Ivy-1.4	-	-	-	-	-	0.933	0.933	0.925	0.933	0.925	0.929	0.94
Ivy-2	-	-	-	-	-	0.897	0.871	0.892	0.880	0.880	0.894	0.894
Jedit-4.1	-	-	-	-	-	0.788	0.785	0.788	0.794	0.766	0.78	0.802
Log4j.1	-	-	-	-	-	0.796	0.76	0.779	0.8	0.740	0.761	0.778
Lucene2.2	-	-	-	-	-	0.627	0.587	0.587	0.628	0.547	0.581	0.639
Poi2.5	-	-	-	-	-	0.763	0.753	0.781	0.777	0.766	0.762	0.78
Poi3.0	-	-	-	-	-	0.760	0.762	0.780	0.734	0.751	0.699	0.748
Synapse1.2	-	-	-	-	-	0.714	0.695	0.710	0.671	0.699	0.725	0.715
Xerces1.3	-	-	-	-	-	0.869	0.858	0.856	0.858	0.863	0.839	0.865

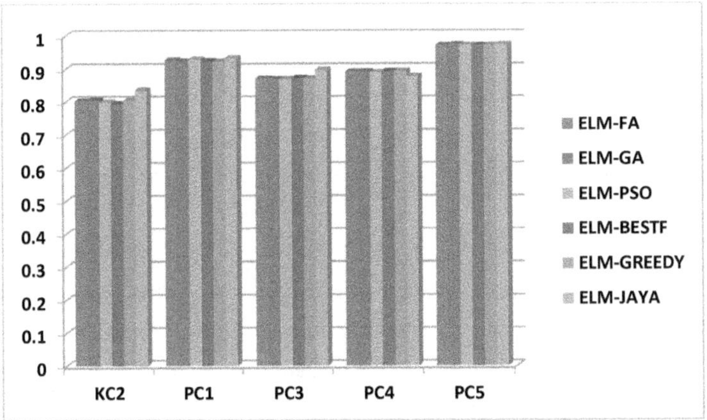

Fig. 3.4 Comparison graph of ELM-JAYA hybrid model

3.6 Chapter Summary and Future Scope

Our study introduces the JAYA-ELM hybrid model as a robust framework for SRP, addressing the challenges of feature selection and computational efficiency. By integrating the Jaya optimization algorithm with Extreme Learning Machine (ELM), our approach demonstrates superior predictive accuracy compared to established methodologies in SRP. Our empirical analysis, detailed in the results comparison section, showcases the efficacy of our JAYA-ELM model across various datasets, including those from NASA and the Java repository. Notably, our model consistently outperforms baseline techniques in prediction accuracy. For instance, in datasets like KC2 and MW1, our model achieved significantly higher accuracies compared to alternative methodologies, indicating notable performance enhancement. The comparative findings underscore the practical utility of our hybrid model, highlighting the efficacy of feature selection techniques in improving predictive performance. By reducing training time and enhancing accuracy, our framework provides a refined approach to software reliability estimation. Moving forward, research may explore further optimization strategies and model refinement to address evolving challenges in software engineering comprehensively. Overall, our study contributes valuable methodological insights, offering practitioners an effective tool for accurate and efficient SRP. In the current study, we have not addressed the imbalance nature of the dataset; however, this will be a focus of future research, where we plan to implement techniques such as oversampling and undersampling to manage dataset imbalance. Moving forward, future research endeavors will also explore further optimization strategies and model refinement to comprehensively tackle evolving challenges in software engineering. Overall, our study contributes methodological insights to the field, providing practitioners with an effective tool for accurate and efficient SRP.

3.6.1 Challenges

The challenges in this model included addressing imbalanced datasets, where minority classes are underrepresented, which can be mitigated through ensemble learning techniques like bagging, boosting, or cost-sensitive ensembles. Feature selection and dimensionality reduction remain critical, as identifying optimal subsets can be improved using ensemble methods such as RF feature importance or recursive feature elimination. Generalization across diverse datasets highlights the need for scalable and adaptable models, which heterogeneous ensembles can address effectively. Computational efficiency is another challenge, as the training time for feature selection and optimization increases with dataset complexity, and methods like gradient boosting or efficient bagging can help reduce this. Overfitting in high-dimensional data is a concern, which ensemble techniques with regularization, such as AdaBoost or gradient boosting, can minimize. Parameter tuning for hybrid models like JAYA-ELM is computationally intensive, but stacking methods in ensemble learning can leverage multiple algorithms without excessive tuning. Scalability remains crucial as software systems grow in complexity, and distributed frameworks like XGBoost can handle large datasets efficiently. Finally, hybrid models often lack interpretability, but ensemble methods like decision tree ensembles or explainable boosting machines (EBMs) can enhance transparency and trust in predictions, making them more suitable for practical applications in software engineering.

CHAPTER:4 Optimal Feature Selection through Jaya Optimization Integrated with Ensemble Learning and SMOTE

4.1 Introduction

Analyzing software defect data poses several challenges, including feature irrelevance, missing samples, redundancy, and correlation [159]. Another common issue is maintaining a balanced distribution between defective and non-defective software data, as the non-defective class often dominates in many experimental settings. This study aims to demonstrate the effectiveness of combining Ensemble learning (EL) with Feature selection (FS) to improve defect classification performance. To address issues such as feature redundancy and data imbalance, we propose a novel EL approach that enhances robustness during classification [160]. By integrating efficient feature selection with ensemble models, the negative impact on fault classification is minimized. Forward selection results indicate that a small subset of features can account for a significant portion of the area under the receiver operating curve (AUC). When comparing feature selection methods, Greedy forward selection (GFS) outperformed Pearson's correlation approach on the datasets. EL, RF and the proposed Average probability ensemble (APE), demonstrate greater resilience to weak feature influence compared to W-SVMs and ELM. In experiments with NASA and Java datasets, the enhanced average probability ensemble model, combined with GFS, achieved exceptionally high accuracy, with the AUC approaching 1.0, reflecting outstanding predictive performance.

This study highlights the significance of carefully selecting features in a software dataset to achieve accurate defect classification. The proposed ensemble learning model effectively addressed challenges inherent in software data and demonstrated strong classification performance. Various methodologies in software engineering focus on predicting critical factors essential for project success [161]. One study presents a comprehensive literature review on the application of machine learning techniques for software effort estimation. It also evaluates their empirical effectiveness across various experimental settings. Another investigation evaluates models for predicting effort in software maintenance tasks, offering insights from practical implementations. Additional research synthesizes studies on software maintainability prediction, identifying common metrics and assessing their predictive value. Moreover, multivariate adaptive regression splines have been explored to forecast the maintainability of object-oriented software. Transfer learning techniques have been applied to cross-company SDP, enhancing prediction accuracy across different organizational contexts [162]. Practical applications of statistical methods in reliability prediction have also been examined, including a case study from the Turkish telecommunications industry that provides real-world insights. Fuzzy clustering techniques are employed in software quality prediction to categorize projects and forecast quality levels [163]. Finally, a critical assessment of SDP models is presented, discussing both their strengths and areas requiring improvement.

Fault-prone software modules have a significant impact on customer satisfaction, development costs and maintenance efforts [164]. To address this, an innovative strategy for SDP has been proposed using weighted classification through association rule mining, which enhances prediction accuracy by assigning greater importance to key features. A systematic examination of just-in-time SDP, summarizing the techniques and methodologies used in this field, forms a central part of the research [165]. In a related area, Bayesian methods have been applied to integrate high-frequency sensor data into watershed water quality modeling, demonstrating the usefulness of probabilistic approaches in environmental assessments [166]. Similarly, Bayesian approaches in SDP provide insights into probabilistic modeling techniques. Furthermore, a hybrid model combining residual NN and long short-term memory architectures has been proposed for automatic modulation classification, achieving precise classification results [167]. However, these methods often underperform when confronted with redundant or skewed defect datasets [168]. Prediction accuracy can decline due to missing or irrelevant information in defect datasets [169], and classifiers such as ANN-MLPs and SVMs tend to produce high false-negative rates because of bias toward the dominant class.

Ensemble learning techniques are better suited to address these challenges. Although not specifically designed for imbalanced data, RFs outperform many other methods in identifying defective modules. The negative impact of irrelevant and redundant features is mitigated through the voting mechanism in ensemble learning, where classifiers that perform better on testing datasets are given more weight. This approach helps improve prediction accuracy by tolerating noise and irrelevant features, ultimately enhancing overall classification performance [170]. The proposed system in this study employs eight classifiers: Bernoulli Naive Bayes (BNB), Gradient

Boosting (GB), WSVM, RF, SGD, ELM, Logistic Regression (LR), and Multinomial Naive Bayes (MNB) [171]. These base classifiers were selected following rigorous simulation validation. The literature identifies classifiers such as WSVMs and RF as standard choices. Because the classification capabilities of individual base classifiers vary, their combination in an ensemble learning approach is particularly effective, capturing a wide range of statistical features inherent in the underlying data [172]. To achieve the study objectives, two hypotheses are proposed. The first hypothesis states that the performance of defect classification models is highly sensitive to the choice of feature subsets, with irrelevant and redundant features negatively affecting predictive accuracy. The second hypothesis suggests that the proposed APE algorithm surpasses existing single and ensemble classifiers, particularly for software defect datasets affected by class imbalance and feature redundancy.

4.2 Problem Formulation

The aim of this study is to improve SRP by combining ensemble learning techniques with feature selection, applied to both imbalanced and balanced datasets. Software reliability is a crucial factor that affects the success and maintenance costs of software systems. However, accurately predicting reliability is challenging due to issues such as data imbalance, feature redundancy, and irrelevant features. The primary goal is to develop a robust prediction model capable of handling imbalanced datasets, minimizing the impact of irrelevant and redundant features, and achieving high predictive accuracy. Key challenges include data imbalance, which can cause biased predictions and poor generalization; feature redundancy and irrelevance, which can reduce model performance; and high dimensionality, which increases computational complexity and the risk of overfitting. To address these challenges, the study integrates ensemble learning techniques that are naturally resilient to class imbalance and improves predictive performance through effective feature selection methods such as greedy forward selection and Pearson's correlation. The approach is evaluated on both imbalanced and balanced datasets.

The methodology involves collecting and preprocessing software defect datasets, implementing and assessing FS techniques, developing ensemble learning models including RF and the APE, and evaluating model performance using metrics such as AUC-ROC, accuracy, precision, recall, and F1-score. Comparative analysis is conducted to validate the effectiveness of the models on imbalanced versus balanced datasets. The expected outcomes include a reliable SRP model capable of handling data imbalance, reducing the effects of irrelevant and redundant features, improving predictive accuracy and generalization, and providing insights into effective FS and EL strategies. By addressing these challenges, the study aims to contribute to the field of software engineering by offering a dependable approach for predicting software reliability, ultimately enhancing software quality and lowering maintenance costs. The proposed framework aims to deliver higher prediction accuracy, resilience to data imbalance, and better generalization across varied software datasets. The key contribution is summarized as follows:

- Proposed a novel hybrid EL framework that integrates SMOTE for handling class imbalance and a Modified Jaya Optimization Algorithm for selecting the most relevant features.
- Incorporated eight diverse classifiers (ELM, RF, W-SVM, GB, LR, SGD, BNB, and MNB) combined through average probability voting to enhance predictive performance.
- Enhanced the Jaya Optimization Algorithm with adaptive control parameters to improve convergence speed and avoid local optima in feature selection.
- Conducted comprehensive experiments on six widely-used PROMISE datasets (PC2, PC4, MC1, KC3, Camel-1.6, and Ant-1.7) using 10-fold cross-validation to ensure generalizability.
- Validated the robustness, adaptability, and practical utility of the proposed framework in real-world SRP scenarios.

4.3 Proposed Model Architecture and Methodology

This study develops a set of classifiers designed to support the challenging task of identifying resilient software defects, with APE serving as the central framework. Multiple base classifiers are combined through EL to build robust models that effectively address common issues in software defect datasets, such as feature redundancy and data imbalance. By integrating classification outputs from diverse classifiers, the model achieves enhanced resilience. Unlike traditional voting methods, classifiers that produce probability outputs use the Area under the ROC curve to measure the confidence of predicted classes, allowing for a more accurate assessment of probabilistic predictions. Voting systems typically require a strict cutoff point for making classification decisions, which can sometimes result in incorrect outcomes. To address this limitation, the mean probability ensemble approach is adopted, which aligns with Area AUC parameters and eliminates the need for threshold selection. In the proposed APE model, each classifier estimates the likelihood that a software component belongs to the defective class, and the final prediction is obtained by averaging these probabilities. The ensemble incorporates eight base classifiers, including ELM, RF, W-SVM, GB, LR, SGD, BNB, and MNB, chosen for their wide acceptance in both artificial intelligence research and software development practice. The model leverages various classification approaches, including statistical, neural, clustering, decision tree, and SVM techniques. Empirical results from the study confirm the effectiveness of the selected base classifiers in enhancing the performance of the EL approach.

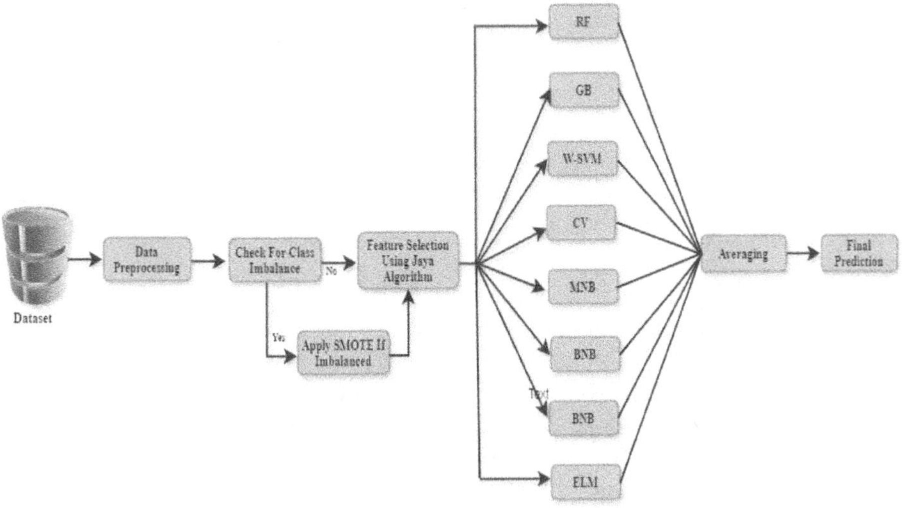

Fig. 4.1 Proposed ensemble model based on average probabilities

4.3.1 Data description and Preprocessing

All computational experiments in this study were carried out on a Windows 10 PC with 32 GB of RAM and an octa-core CPU operating at 3.6 GHz. A 10-fold cross-validation technique was used to evaluate the models. The performance of each classifier was analyzed using individual software defect datasets, with all algorithms implemented in Python. Classification effectiveness was measured using the AUC, which is particularly suitable for evaluating classifiers on imbalanced datasets [173]. Basic classifiers, including WSVMs, ELM, and RF, were employed as benchmarks to assess the proposed APE approach. To address the study objectives, several FS methods, such as Pearson's correlation, GFS, and Fisher's criterion, were evaluated. The classification performance of the proposed APE model was tested using six publicly available software defect datasets, including Ant-1.7 and Camel-1.6 from the Java Repository and KC3, MC1, PC2, and PC4 from the NASA Repository. The attributes of these datasets, along with their abbreviated codes, are summarized in Table 4.1.

Table 4.1 Features used in proposed ensemble model

Features	Code	Features	Code
Decision Count	f1	Node Count	f26
Cyclomatic Complexity	f2	Response for Class	f27
Global Data Density	f3	Measure of functional Abstraction	f28
Halstead Difficulty	f4	Edge Count	f29
Halstead Content	f5	Decision Density	f30
Maintenance Severity	f6	Design Density	f31
Coupling Between Objects	f7	Parameter Count	f32
Number of Unique Operands	f8	Number of Public Methods	f33
Afferent Couplings	f9	Lines of Commented Lines	f34
Essential Density	f10	Lines of Code	f35
Global Data Complexity	f11	Halstead Programming Time	f36
Efferent Couplings	f12	Halstead Level	f37
Lack of Cohesion of Methods	f13	Design Complexity	f38
Condition Count	f14	Call Pairs	f39
Lines of Blank Lines	f15	Lines of Executable Code	f40
Average Method Complexity	f16	Halstead Volume	f41
Number of Children	f17	Lines of Code & Comments	f42
Essential Complexity	f18	Halstead Error Estimate	f45
Measure of Aggregation	f19	Halstead Effort	f46
Percentage of Comments	f20	Cyclomatic Density	f47
Depth of Inheritance Tree	f21	Halstead Length	f48
Coupling Between Modules	f22	Inheritance Coupling	f49
Multiple Condition Count	f23	Cohesion Among Methods	f50
Number of Unique Operators	f24	Data access Metric	f51
Weighted Methods for Class	f25	Maximum Cyclomatic Complexity	f52

4.3.2 Performance Criteria

To evaluate the classification performance of the proposed frameworks and validate the study results, a series of simulations were conducted. These simulations employed a balanced 10-fold cross-validation approach, ensuring that the data was appropriately divided into training and testing sets. Given that software fault datasets are often time-consuming and costly to obtain, using 10-fold cross-validation helps reduce biases when testing hypotheses. Balanced sampling was applied to maintain an equitable distribution of fault-free and defective classes within each fold, ensuring that both classes were represented in similar proportions. This method preserves the class imbalance ratio and allows for a more accurate assessment of model performance.

To test the first hypothesis, the dataset was initially split into 70 percent for training and 30 percent for testing. An empty feature list, denoted as li, was created. Based on a chosen feature selection criterion, the most relevant feature from the training set was identified and added to li. The ensemble classifiers were then trained using the selected features, and the trained models were applied to the test set to identify defective instances. The resulting performance metrics were recorded. This process was repeated by iteratively selecting additional features and updating the performance data, highlighting inconsistencies in classification performance caused by feature selection and thereby validating the first hypothesis. For the second hypothesis, the dataset was again split with 70 percent for training and 30 percent for testing. The proposed model was trained on the training set and evaluated on the test set, with its classification performance recorded as f1. The greedy forward selection method was then applied to the training data to identify the most relevant features, which were added to the li list. Using this updated feature set, the APE model was retrained and its performance on the test set was recorded as f2. Comparing f1 and f2 demonstrates the superiority of the proposed ensemble model in handling imbalanced and redundant data, thereby supporting the second hypothesis.

In the proposed Optimal Feature Selection through Jaya Optimization Integrated with Ensemble Learning and SMOTE, the performance of the classification models is evaluated using standard metrics derived from the confusion matrix. Accuracy, which measures the overall correctness of the model, is defined as $\text{Accuracy} = \frac{TP+TN}{TP+TN+FP+FN}$ (4.1) where TP, TN, FP, and FN represent true positives, true negatives, false positives, and false negatives, respectively. Precision, indicating the reliability of positive predictions, is calculated as Precision= $\frac{TP}{TP+FP}$ (4.2)

Recall, also referred to as Sensitivity, evaluates the ability of the model to correctly identify actual positive instances and is given by Recall = Sensitivity = $\frac{TP}{TP+FN}$ (4.3)

Specificity, which measures the correct identification of negative instances, is computed as Specificity = $1 - \frac{FP}{TN+FN}$ (4.4)

The F-Measure (F1-score) provides a harmonic balance between precision and recall and is expressed as F1 = $\frac{2\ X\ Precision\ X\ Sensitivity}{Precision + Sensitivity}$ (4.5)

Additionally, the G-Mean, which reflects the balance between sensitivity and specificity and is particularly suitable for imbalanced datasets even after SMOTE application, is defined as

G-mean = $\sqrt{Specificity * Sensitivity}$ (4.6)

Collectively, these evaluation metrics ensure a robust and unbiased assessment of the Jaya-optimized feature subsets integrated with ensemble learning models trained on SMOTE-balanced data.

4.3.3 Algorithmic Workflow of the Proposed Methods

The oveall proposed algorithms are given in below:

Input:

- *Software defect dataset*
- *Target variable (reliability label)*

Output:

- *Predicted reliability classes*
- *Evaluation metrics (accuracy, precision, recall, f1-score, etc.)*

Step 1: *Data Preprocessing*

1.1. Load the dataset.

1.2. Handle missing values (if any) using imputation or deletion.

1.3. Normalize or standardize numerical features if necessary.

1.4. Encode categorical variables using label encoding or one-hot encoding.
1.5. Split the dataset into features (X) and target labels (y).
Step 2: *Check for Class Imbalance*
2.1. Calculate the distribution of class labels.
2.2. If the class distribution is imbalanced:
2.2.1. Apply SMOTE (Synthetic Minority Oversampling Technique) to balance the dataset.
2.2.2. Re-split the balanced data into training and testing sets.
Step 3: *feature Selection using Modified Jaya Optimization Algorithm*
3.1. Initialize a population of candidate solutions (feature subsets).
3.2. Define a fitness function based on classifier performance (e.g., accuracy or f1-score).
3.3. for each generation:
  3.3.1. Evaluate the fitness of each solution.
  3.3.2. Update each solution using the modified Jaya Algorithm equation:

$$X'_{i,k,l} = X_{i,k,l} + \omega \cdot \left[r_{1,i,l}\left(X_{i,best,l} - X_{i,k,l}\right)\right] - \left[r_{2,i,l}\left(X_{i,worst,l} - X_{i,k,l}\right)\right]$$

  Where:
  - w is a linearly decreasing weight (exploration to exploitation)
  - r_1, r_2 are random numbers in [0,1]
  3.3.3. Accept the new solution if its fitness improves.
  3.3.4. Repeat until convergence or maximum iterations.
3.4. Select the best feature subset found by modified Jaya Algorithm.
Step 4: *Train Base Classifiers Using Selected features*
4.1. Use the optimized feature subset to train the following base classifiers:-
(ELM, Rf, W-SVM, GB, LR, SGD, BNB and MNB)
Step 5: *Ensemble Model Using Averaging*
5.1. Predict output probabilities or labels using all 8 base classifiers.
5.2. Compute the average of predicted probabilities or labels.
5.3. Apply a threshold (e.g., 0.5) to finalize the predicted class.
Step 6: *Evaluate the Ensemble Model*
6.1. Use the test dataset to evaluate model performance.
6.2. Compute evaluation metrics: (Accuracy, Precision, Recall, f1-Score, Specificity)
Step 7: *Output the Prediction Results and Metrics*

4.4 Comparative Performance Evaluation of APE and Enhanced APE (EAPE) with W-SVM, RF, and ELM

The proposed enhanced APE approach integrates seven core classifiers, and the probabilities generated by these classifiers are averaged to determine the final classification outcome. Using the selected datasets, the performance of Weighted SVMs and RF classifiers was compared with that of the Average Probability Ensemble model, focusing on preprocessing and feature selection. Table 4.2 compares the AUC values of various classifiers. The proposed APE model achieved the highest AUC value of 0.83, surpassing WSVMs at 0.80 and RF at 0.78, consistent with the second hypothesis. This result demonstrates that the ensemble approach is more effective than WSVMs, which are specifically designed for imbalanced datasets, highlighting the strength of ensemble methods in software defect classification.

For the PC2 dataset, the APE model demonstrated a remarkable AUC of 0.92, successfully distinguishing between classes, whereas WSVMs and RF achieved only 0.54 and 0.74, respectively. This highlights that although WSVMs are included as base classifiers within the ensemble, their individual performance does not reduce the overall effectiveness of the model. The results in Table 4.3 further support the second hypothesis, showing that ensemble learning outperforms individual classifiers in classification accuracy, particularly when base classifiers are selected for their proven performance. Moreover, the inclusion of lower-performing base classifiers does not adversely impact the ensemble's overall results, confirming and validating the second hypothesis.

Table 4.2 Performance of W-SVMs, RF, ELM, and APE Models

Datasets	W-SVMs	RF	ELM	APE
Ant-1.7	0.78	0.80	0.81	0.83
Camel-1.6	0.60	0.68	0.69	0.73
PC4	0.66	0.87	0.89	0.90
PC2	0.54	0.74	0.75	0.92
MC1	0.81	0.84	0.85	0.88
KC3	0.53	0.67	0.68	0.76

It incorporating a FS module into the proposed APE model proves valuable due to the positive impact of FS on classification performance. The enhanced APE (EAPE) model focuses exclusively on fault-relevant indicators, which are expected to improve prediction accuracy. FS is carried out using the GFS approach, which outperforms other selection techniques. Table 4.3 presents the classification performance of the original APE model alongside its upgraded version, highlighting the improvements achieved through GFS. When applied across all defect datasets, the augmented model consistently outperformed the basic APE model. This improvement is attributed to the forward greedy selection method, which prioritizes relevant and informative software metrics while eliminating redundant and irrelevant features. The impact of enhancing the APE model, referred to as EAPE, is evaluated by comparing its classification accuracy with the original APE model. Results show a consistent increase in accuracy across all datasets when using EAPE. For example, in the PC2 dataset, accuracy improves from 0.92 in APE to 0.94 with EAPE, reflecting optimized performance. Similarly, accuracy rises from 0.88 to 0.91 in the MC1 dataset and from 0.73 to 0.77 in the Camel-1.6 dataset. This trend is observed across all evaluated datasets, demonstrating that the enhancements successfully improve classification performance. Overall, EAPE emerges as a more refined and reliable version of APE, making it a stronger choice for SRP.

Table 4.3 Evaluation of APE and EAPE Models

Datasets	APE	Enhanced APE (EAPE)
Ant-1.7	0.83	0.85
Camel-1.6	0.73	0.77
PC4	0.90	0.92
PC2	0.92	0.94
MC1	0.88	0.91
KC3	0.76	0.80

The effectiveness of existing algorithms such as WSVMs and RF is analyzed in relation to the impact of feature selection. Table 4.4 presents the performance of the proposed enhanced algorithm along with improved versions of RF, WSVM, and ELM classifiers. FS helps improve classification performance for both the proposed and existing classifiers, supporting the first hypothesis. The improved WSVM and RF classifiers performed as expected, showing noticeable gains. In addition, the enhanced Average Probability Ensemble model, referred to as EAPE, outperformed the improved versions of the other classifiers. In classification tasks with imbalanced datasets, the geometric mean is often used to measure performance. The comparison is expanded to include all improved models including EAPE, enhanced WSVM, enhanced RF, and enhanced ELM to determine whether improvements lead to higher classification accuracy. The results clearly show that EAPE consistently outperforms all other models, maintaining the highest accuracy across all datasets. For example, in the PC2 dataset, EAPE achieves an accuracy of 0.94, which is considerably higher than the enhanced WSVM at 0.58, enhanced RF at 0.76, and enhanced ELM at 0.81. In the PC4 dataset, EAPE reaches 0.92, surpassing the enhanced WSVM at 0.69, enhanced RF at 0.90, and enhanced ELM at 0.91. Even in datasets with smaller differences, such as Ant 1.7, EAPE remains the most effective model with an accuracy of 0.85 compared to 0.81 for the enhanced RF and 0.82 for the enhanced ELM. This evaluation metric demonstrates the classifier's ability to accurately classify both minority and majority classes, as it combines sensitivity and specificity, capturing the following aspects.

Table 4.4 AUC Measure Comparison of EAPE, W-SVMs, RF, and ELM

Datasets	EAPE	Enhanced W-SVMs	Enhanced RF	Enhanced ELM
Ant-1.7	0.85	0.80	0.81	0.82
Camel-1.6	0.77	0.63	0.70	0.72
PC4	0.92	0.69	0.90	0.91
PC2	0.94	0.58	0.76	0.81
MC1	0.91	0.83	0.85	0.87
KC3	0.80	0.69	0.71	0.73

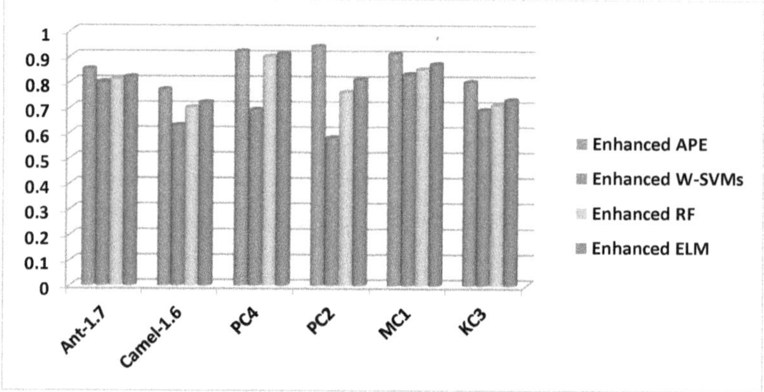

Fig. 4.2 Result comparison between APE, W-SVMs, RF, ELM models

Table 4.5 presents a comprehensive overview of the classification results for the proposed ensemble learning approach using a multivariate method. The table also compares the performance of the original and enhanced versions of existing algorithms based on the G-mean metric. The classification accuracy of different machine learning models, including WSVM, RF, ELM, and Adaptive Prediction Error, along with their enhanced versions, is reported across six datasets: Ant-1.7, Camel-1.6, PC4, PC2, MC1, and KC3. The results demonstrate that the proposed APE model and its enhanced version consistently achieve the highest accuracy across all datasets. For example, in the PC2 dataset, standard models perform poorly, with Weighted SVMs, RF, ELM, and APE showing an accuracy of zero. In contrast, EAPE significantly improves performance, reaching an accuracy of 0.90. Similarly, in the Ant-1.7 dataset, standard APE achieves an accuracy of 0.78, which increases to 0.83 with Enhanced APE. This trend is observed across all datasets, indicating that the enhanced versions of the models improve classification performance, with Enhanced APE leading in accuracy. The G-mean metric effectively evaluates the impact of data imbalance on classification performance. Low G-mean values indicate poor handling of minority class information, as seen with the Weighted SVM classifier in the PC2, KC3, and Ant-1.7 datasets. The RF classifier showed similar behavior, especially in the PC2 dataset. The enhanced APE model outperformed all previous classifiers, achieving the highest classification accuracy and a perfect G-mean score of one. This represents one of the highest reported accuracies in the literature for software defect datasets when evaluated using the G-mean metric.

Table 4.5 G-mean Measure comparison of EAPE with other models

Datasets	W-SVMs	RF	ELM	APE	Enhanced W-SVMs	Enhanced RF	Enhanced ELM	Enhanced APE
Ant-1.7	0	0.63	0.76	0.78	0.79	0.80	0.81	0.83
Camel-1.6	0.33	0.36	0.45	0.65	0.69	0.71	0.73	0.75
PC4	0.07	0.52	0.61	0.78	0.81	0.84	0.87	0.89
PC2	0	0	0	0	0.81	0.83	0.85	0.90
MC1	0.324	0.41	0.53	0.68	0.79	0.82	0.85	0.88
KC3	0	0.25	0.46	0.71	0.73	0.76	0.76	0.78

4.5 Performance Evaluation of Proposed Model

Table 4.6 provides a detailed comparison of three ensemble learning techniques evaluated using ten-fold cross-validation across six software defect datasets: PC4, MC1, KC3, PC2, Camel1.6, and Ant1.7. The methods assessed include the APE Approach, its GFS-based variant (GFS-APE), and the Jaya-based variant (Jaya APE). Performance was measured across five key metrics: accuracy, f-measure, precision, recall, and specificity, offering a comprehensive view of each approach's classification capability and robustness. For the PC4 dataset, APE achieved an accuracy of 0.90 along with an f-measure of 0.87. Its precision and recall were 0.83 and 0.86

respectively, while specificity reached 0.85. GFS APE improved these values, increasing accuracy to 0.92, f-measure to 0.90, precision to 0.89, and recall to 0.87, although specificity slightly decreased to 0.83. Jaya APE performed the best, achieving an accuracy of 0.97, f-measure of 0.95, precision of 0.93, recall of 0.94, and a specificity of 0.91, indicating its strong ability to classify both defective and non-defective instances effectively. The results from the MC1 dataset followed a similar trend. APE scored 0.88 in accuracy and 0.83 in f-measure, with precision at 0.82 and recall at 0.77. Specificity remained lower at 0.79. GFS-APE showed improvements, reaching 0.91 in accuracy and 0.88 in f-measure, with precision and recall increasing to 0.89 and 0.86, and specificity improving to 0.85. Jaya APE again delivered the strongest results, with accuracy of 0.97, f-measure of 0.90, precision at 0.87, recall at 0.95, and specificity of 0.90, demonstrating a well-balanced performance.

For the KC3 dataset, differences among the models were more pronounced. APE scored 0.76 in accuracy and 0.74 in f-measure, with precision and recall close to 0.75 and 0.73, and specificity at 0.70. GFS-APE slightly improved these values, achieving 0.80 in accuracy, 0.79 in f-measure, 0.76 in precision, 0.80 in recall, and 0.79 in specificity. Jaya APE showed a notable improvement, reaching 0.89 in accuracy, 0.91 in f-measure, 0.90 in precision, 0.87 in recall, and 0.89 in specificity, highlighting its effectiveness in handling complex or noisy data. For the PC2 dataset, APE already delivered strong baseline results, with accuracy at 0.92, f-measure at 0.86, precision at 0.88, recall at 0.83, and specificity at 0.85. GFS-APE provided slight improvements, increasing accuracy to 0.94 and f-measure to 0.91, with precision rising to 0.93 and recall to 0.89, although specificity decreased to 0.82. Jaya APE maintained its leading performance, with accuracy at 0.96, f-measure at 0.95, precision at 0.85, recall at 0.89, and specificity improving to 0.91. Despite a small reduction in precision, the method sustained strong overall performance with a high f-measure.

Camel1.6 dataset proves to be one of the more challenging datasets. The APE model records its lowest performance on this dataset, achieving an accuracy of 0.73 and an f-measure of 0.72. Its precision drops to 0.69, recall to 0.71, and specificity to 0.65. GFS-APEL provides modest improvements across most metrics, with accuracy increasing to 0.77, f-measure to 0.73, recall to 0.76, and specificity to 0.76, although precision declines slightly to 0.65. Jaya APE delivers a significant improvement, raising accuracy to 0.83, f-measure to 0.81, precision to 0.83, recall to 0.79, and specificity to 0.84, demonstrating its ability to handle lower quality or more challenging data effectively. Ant1.7 dataset shows more balanced performance across all models. APE achieves an accuracy of 0.83, f-measure of 0.79, precision of 0.81, recall of 0.75, and specificity of 0.82. GFS-APE improves slightly, with accuracy reaching 0.85 and f-measure at 0.84, while precision and recall remain at 0.81 and 0.75, and specificity remains stable at 0.82. Jaya APE consistently performs the best, achieving an accuracy of 0.89, f-measure of 0.85, precision and recall both at 0.86, and specificity improving to 0.87.

Across all six datasets, the Average Probability Ensemble Learning Approach establishes solid baseline results. Both optimization-driven variants, however, consistently outperform the baseline model. GFS-APE provides moderate gains, though it occasionally sacrifices precision or specificity. Jaya-APE emerges as the most effective method overall, consistently achieving high scores in critical metrics such as recall and f-measure, which are essential for identifying software defects. This demonstrates that the approach is not only accurate but also reliable across datasets with different characteristics and levels of complexity. The integration of optimization algorithms into ensemble learning clearly adds value, and the Jaya-based enhancements offer robust improvements, making them particularly suitable for real-world SDP tasks. Figure 4.3 provides a visual comparison of the performance of all ensemble methods.

Table 4.6 Result of our proposed model

10 fold Cross Validation	Input		PC4	MC1	KC3	PC2	Camel1.6	Ant1.7
	Average Probability Ensemble Learning Approach	Accuracy	0.9	0.88	0.76	0.92	0.73	0.83
		F-Measure	0.87	0.83	0.74	0.86	0.72	0.79
		Precision	0.83	0.82	0.75	0.88	0.69	0.81
		Recall	0.86	0.77	0.73	0.83	0.71	0.75
		Specificity	0.85	0.79	0.7	0.85	0.65	0.82
	GfS Based - Average Probability Ensemble Learning Approach	Accuracy	0.92	0.91	0.8	0.94	0.77	0.85
		F-Measure	0.9	0.88	0.79	0.91	0.73	0.84
		Precision	0.89	0.89	0.76	0.93	0.65	0.81
		Recall	0.87	0.86	0.8	0.89	0.76	0.75
		Specificity	0.83	0.85	0.79	0.82	0.76	0.82
	Jaya Based- Average Probability Ensemble Learning Approach	Accuracy	0.97	0.97	0.89	0.96	0.83	0.89
		F-Measure	0.95	0.9	0.91	0.95	0.81	0.85
		Precision	0.93	0.87	0.9	0.85	0.83	0.86
		Recall	0.94	0.95	0.87	0.89	0.79	0.86
		Specificity	0.91	0.9	0.89	0.91	0.84	0.87

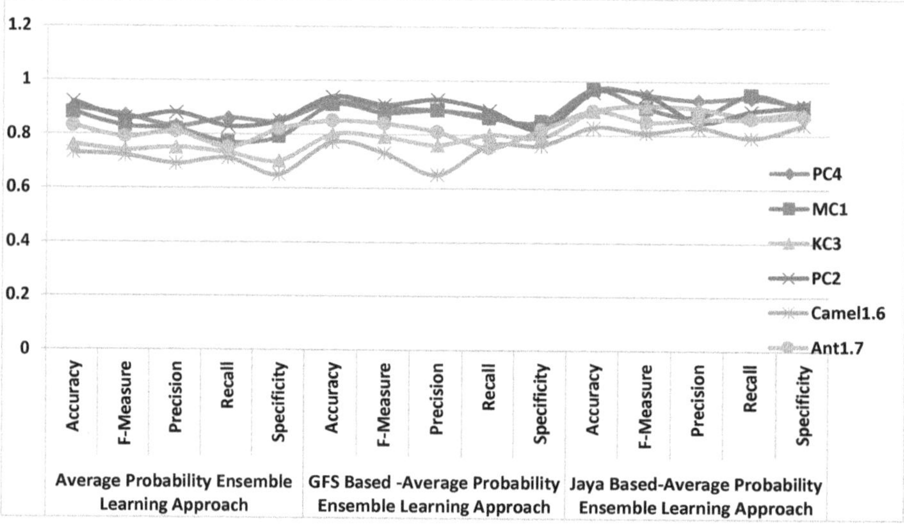

Fig. 4.3 Analysis of results from different approaches

4.6 Results and Discussions

Table 4.7 presents the feature selection results for six widely used software defect datasets, including Ant-1.7, Camel-1.6, PC4, PC2, MC1, and KC3. The evaluation considers four enhanced classification models: Weighted SVMs, RFs, ELMs, and APE. Each model was likely optimized using algorithms such as Jaya to improve prediction accuracy by selecting the most relevant software metrics, ranging from f1 to f51, which may represent complexity, coupling, inheritance, or other software attributes. For the Ant-1.7 dataset, Weighted SVMs selected a minimal set of features, including f49, f16, f13, and f20, while RFs and ELM chose broader, overlapping sets. APE incorporated an even larger collection of features, reflecting the trade-off between simplicity and comprehensive representation. In the Camel-1.6 dataset, there was more convergence across models, with features such as f9, f13, f21, and f28 frequently selected, indicating their strong predictive relevance. The PC4 dataset displayed wider variation, but features like f31 and f36 were consistently chosen, highlighting their importance.

For PC2, many features, including f1, f8, f24, and f26, were shared among models, suggesting partial agreement, while APE again extended coverage. MC1 showed diverse feature selections, yet features such as f36 and f40 were commonly selected, indicating high predictive power. KC3 demonstrated the highest agreement among models, consistently highlighting f2, f18, f23, f36, and f43 as important. Overall, the results indicate that enhanced models are capable of identifying both dataset-specific and universally significant features. APE generally captured a wider range of features, whereas Weighted SVMs tended to favor smaller, more compact subsets. This comparison highlights the influence of model architecture and optimization on feature relevance and selection, offering valuable insights for defect prediction strategies and future feature engineering efforts.

Table 4.7 AUC-based features of proposed ensemble model

Dataset	Enhanced W-SVMs	Enhanced RF	Enhanced ELM	Enhanced APE
Ant-1.7	f49 f16 f13 f16	f25 f28 f49 f17 f36 f22 f21 f35 f16	f25 f28 f49 f17 f36 f22 f21 f35 f16 f49 f16 f13 f16 f20	f28 f17 f48 f13 f50 f19 f51 f29 f36 f12 f22 f49 f35 f25 f34 f21 f9 f16 f20
Camel-1.6	f13 f35 f51 f22 f17 f21 f16 f28 f12 f16	f9 f16 f49 f21 f29 f13 f34 f12 f19 f28 f22	f9 f16 f49 f21 f13 f35 f51 f22 f29 f13 f34 f12	f9 f13 f51 f21 f29 f34 f17 f22 f17 f24
PC4	f43 f2 f15 f6 f31 f14 f10 f26 f2 f46 f38 f18 f31 f36	f43 f14 f2 f15 f36 f20 f39 f33 f38 f35 f42 f24	f36 f20 f39 f33 f14 f10 f26 f2 f46 f38 f18 f31 f36	f43 f15 f24 f31 f18 f40 f33 f5 f35 f44 f41 f36 f39 f26 f14 f16
PC2	f37 f24 f44 f41 f24 f8 f1 f23 f26 f20	f38 f20 f8 f26 f45 f5 f2 f36 f40 f1 f37 f33	f24 f8 f1 f23 f26 f5 f2 f36 f40 f1 f37 f33 f20	f45 f37 f24 f20 f43 f10 f36 f39
MC1	f36 f20 f47 f4 f26 f40 f36 f43 f30 f27	f36 f20 f15 f46 f30 f1 f18 f8 f27 f33 f24 f40 f31 f41 f14 f6 f2 f36	f30 f1 f18 f8 f27 f33 f24 f40 f31 f40 f36 f43 f30	f20 f2 f31 f14 f39 f46 f43 f40 f1 f18 f44 f11 f3 f38 f33 f8 f2
KC3	f2 f43 f18 f33 f6 f11 f32 f36	f43 f24 f44 f10 f23 f36	f23 f36 f11 f32 f36 f2 f43 f18	f2 f43 f18 f33 f23 f36 f39 f42

The impact of feature selection on classification performance was evaluated by comparing two techniques: GFS and the Modified Jaya Optimization Algorithm (MJOA). The comparison was conducted using six widely studied software defect datasets: PC4, MC1, KC3, PC2, Camel-1.6, and Ant-1.7. These datasets differ in programming language, number of components, and defect density, providing a diverse benchmark for analysis. GFS is a traditional wrapper-based approach that sequentially adds features based on observed improvements in performance, whereas the Jaya algorithm is a lightweight, nature-inspired optimizer that iteratively refines feature subsets by moving toward better solutions while avoiding poorer ones. For the Ant-1.7 dataset, which includes 745 Java components and 166 defects, GFS identified 19 relevant features such as f28, f17, f48, f13, and f50. MJOA selected a smaller, more targeted set of 10 features, including f28, f19, f51, f13, and f48. This represents a 47 percent reduction in feature count while retaining the most important predictors, demonstrating MJOA's effectiveness in reducing redundancy without compromising performance. In the Camel-1.6 dataset, which has 965 Java components and 188 defects, GFS chose 11 features including f9, f13, f51, f21, and f29, while MJOA extended the list to 13 features by adding f48 and f50, which GFS overlooked.

The broader selection by MJOA indicates its ability to capture useful feature interactions that a purely greedy strategy might miss.

In the PC4 dataset, which contains 1287 C components and 177 defects, the GFS method identified 17 features, including f43, f15, f24, f31, and A18. MJOA reduced this to 10 features, overlapping on key attributes such as f15, f31, f40, f33, and f36. This reduction of 41 percent demonstrates Jaya algorithm's strength in focusing on high-impact variables while eliminating less relevant ones. For the PC2 dataset, containing 1585 C components and 16 defects, GFS highlighted 8 features such as A45, f37, f24, and f20. MJOA produced a slightly different subset, retaining f45, f37, and f36, while also introducing A8 and A1, reflecting its capability to explore underutilized features that may enhance classification. The MC1 dataset, a C++ dataset with 1988 components and 46 defects, saw GFS select 18 features including f20, f2, f31, f14, and f39. MJOA narrowed this to 9 features, retaining overlaps such as f31, f43, and f39, while also including additional features like f6 and f26, demonstrating its broader search capability. In the KC3 dataset, containing 200 Java components and 36 defects, GFS identified features including f2, f43, f18, and f36. MJOA reduced the selection by nearly 40 percent, keeping f8, f43, f20, and f36, again showing its ability to retain essential features while removing less relevant ones. Table 4.8 provides a detailed comparison of the features selected by GFS and MJOA across all six datasets, highlighting the differences in approach and the efficiency of MJOA in achieving a more concise yet effective feature set.

Table 4.8 Performance of feature Selection using GFS vs Jaya optimization

Dataset	GFS-based feature Selection	Modified Jaya optimization based feature Selection
Ant-1.7	f28 f17 f48 f13 f50 f19 f51 f29 f36 f12 f22 f49 f35 f25 f34 f21 f9 f16 f20	f28 f19 f51 f13 f48 f21 f17 f16 f23
Camel-1.6	f9 f13 f51 f21 f29 f34 f17 f22 f17 f24	f29 f34 f21 f48 f28 f25 f19 f9 f12 f50 f16 f36
PC4	f43 f15 f24 f31 f18 f40 f33 f5 f35 f44 f41 f36 f39 f26 f14 f16	f2 f15 f31 f10 f42 f20 f40 f33 f36
PC2	f45 f37 f24 f20 f43 f10 f36 ff39	f45 f37 f8 f41 f1 f36
MC1	f20 f2 f31 f14 f39 f46 f43 f40 f1 f18 f44 f11 f3 f38 f33 f8 f2	f36 f46 f26 f41 f31 f43 f6 f39 f15 f36
KC3	f2 f43 f18 f33 f23 f36 f39 f42	f8 f43 f20 f5 f36

4.7 Result Comparison

Software SRP relies heavily on the accuracy of classification models and the effectiveness of feature selection techniques. In this study, the base and enhanced accuracies reported in Paper1 by Pachariya et al. [173] and Paper2 by William et al. [174] are compared with the results from the proposed model, using six widely adopted datasets: PC4, MC1, KC3, PC2, Camel1.6, and Ant1.7. The evaluation demonstrates that the proposed model consistently delivers more accurate defect predictions. For the PC4 dataset, both papers reported a baseline accuracy of 0.90. Paper1 improved this to 0.92, and Paper2 achieved 0.96 after applying feature selection. The proposed model outperformed both, reaching 0.97, reflecting superior feature selection and robust model performance. In the MC1 dataset, Paper1 increased accuracy from 0.88 to 0.91, while Paper2 achieved a significant improvement from 0.87 to 0.98. The proposed model closely followed with 0.97, maintaining high accuracy with strong consistency. KC3, which is known for its complexity and noisy data, showed improvements from 0.76 to 0.80 in Paper1 and from 0.75 to 0.86 in Paper2. The proposed model recorded 0.89, outperforming both and demonstrating its ability to handle challenging datasets effectively.

For PC2, initial accuracies were 0.92 and 0.91. Paper1 improved this to 0.94 and Paper2 reached 0.95. The proposed model again led slightly, achieving 0.96, highlighting its ability to sustain high accuracy even when baseline results are already strong. Camel1.6, which typically shows lower initial performance, moved from 0.73 to 0.77 in Paper1 and to 0.80 in Paper2. The proposed model surpassed both, reaching 0.83, indicating improved generalization and more effective feature filtering. Ant1.7 recorded gains from 0.83 to 0.85 and from 0.82 to 0.86 in Papers1 and 2, respectively, while the proposed model achieved 0.89, once again outperforming both methods.

These consistent improvements across all datasets highlight the advantage of integrating the Modified Jaya Optimization Algorithm within the ensemble framework. Unlike the other approaches, the proposed model does not rely on fixed control parameters, allowing it to dynamically and efficiently explore the feature space. This flexibility results in superior classification accuracy and better generalization across datasets with varying complexity. The average accuracy improvement across all datasets further demonstrates the strength of the proposed model, with gains over Paper1 ranging from 0.02 to 0.10 and improvements over Paper2 ranging from 0.01 to 0.07. Overall, these results provide strong evidence of the model's generalizability and its potential as a reliable solution for real-world SDP. The combination of an ensemble of classifiers with a parameter-free, intelligent feature selection strategy leads to more accurate and dependable predictions. Future work could explore the integration of deep NN or hybrid optimization techniques [175] to further enhance the model's flexibility and performance on more complex datasets and industrial applications. Table 4.9 presents a side-by-side comparison between the proposed model and other established approaches.

Table 4.9 Result comparison of proposed ensemble model

	Pachariya et al. 2023[173]		William et al. 2023[174]		
Dataset	**Accuracy**	**Enhanced Accuracy**	**Accuracy**	**Enhanced Accuracy**	**Our Proposed Model Accuracy**
PC4	0.9	0.92	0.9	0.96	0.97
MC1	0.88	0.91	0.87	0.98	0.97
KC3	0.76	0.8	0.75	0.86	0.89
PC2	0.92	0.94	0.91	0.95	0.96
Camel1.6	0.73	0.77	0.73	0.8	0.83
Ant1.7	0.83	0.85	0.82	0.86	0.89

4.8 Chapter Summary and Future Scope

This research explored various feature selection methods for SDP, demonstrating that using top-quality features significantly improves the Area Under the ROC curve. The study highlighted the effectiveness of ensemble learning, especially with unbalanced datasets. The proposed APE, comprising eight learners, outperformed conventional methods like ELM, Weighted-SVMs and RF particularly when combined with Greedy forward Selection. This combination achieved high ROC values across multiple datasets. Future research aims to examine alternative feature selection strategies, assess the redundancy in public datasets, and compare with techniques like Linear Discriminant Analysis and Principal Component Analysis. Additionally, integrating more ensemble learners will be explored to enhance predictive performance.

4.8.1 Challenges

After completing this study, we identified several challenges that can be addressed using ANN. In our future work, we plan to utilize time series datasets to tackle these issues. Feature redundancy and irrelevance in defect datasets often reduce classification accuracy and increase computational costs. However, SARIMA can effectively identify temporal patterns, while ANN can learn nonlinear feature interactions, thereby improving overall efficiency. Data imbalance biases models toward the majority class, leading to higher false negative rates, but ANN's ability to learn complex patterns and SARIMA's analysis of historical trends can mitigate this issue. Noisy and missing data degrade predictive performance, but SARIMA's ability to handle temporal dependencies and ANN's adaptability ensure reliable predictions. Achieving scalability across diverse datasets is difficult due to varying characteristics, but ANN's flexibility and SARIMA's statistical modeling create a solution that generalizes well. Weak features negatively impact performance, yet ANN can weigh feature importance effectively, and SARIMA minimizes their influence. High computational costs from resource-intensive models are addressed by splitting tasks: SARIMA handles temporal dependencies while ANN focuses on feature interactions. Generalizing across datasets without extensive fine-tuning is another challenge overcome by combining SARIMA's reliability with ANN's adaptability.

Integrating classifiers into a robust model is complex, but the hybrid framework uses SARIMA for preprocessing and ANN for classification, streamlining the process. Metrics like AUC and G-mean are optimized during training to evaluate performance in imbalanced datasets, and the hybrid model inherently integrates statistical and neural techniques to avoid overfitting and maximize accuracy. This unified approach provides a robust, scalable, and efficient solution for SRP. Time series datasets, which capture sequential data and temporal dependencies, are preferred over normal textual datasets for tasks like SRP, stock market analysis, or weather forecasting. These datasets allow for predictive modeling based on historical data, enabling the detection of trends and seasonality that would be difficult to capture in textual data. For instance, models like SARIMA, ARIMA, and LSTM are designed to forecast future values based on past observations, whereas textual datasets are better suited for tasks like sentiment analysis or document classification. Time series data has a natural structure with consistent time intervals (e.g., daily or hourly), making it ideal for time-based analysis, while textual data requires different processing methods such as tokenization and word embeddings. Therefore, time series data is critical when modeling dynamic processes over time, whereas textual data is focused on extracting meaning from content.

CHAPTER:5 Improving Software Reliability Prediction with a Hybrid ANN-SARIMA Model Enhanced by Jaya Optimization

5.1 Introduction

Software plays a critical role in running scientific and commercial systems, as well as everyday devices such as phones, televisions, and cars. In high-stakes domains like medical equipment or transportation control systems, software faults can range from minor inconveniences to potentially life-threatening situations [176]. Moreover, software defects increase the risk of data breaches and cyber-attacks, jeopardizing user security and privacy. To mitigate these risks, software development teams must follow rigorous testing procedures, including unit, integration, and system testing. Detecting and fixing problems often requires post-deployment updates and continuous monitoring [177]. However, these measures can be both costly and time-consuming, making accurate reliability assessment essential for effective budget and resource management. Software reliability refers to the ability of software systems to function accurately and efficiently under specified conditions over a certain period of time [178]. It represents the probability that a software system will operate without failure within a given context. Ensuring software reliability involves proper design, development, testing, deployment, and ongoing maintenance. Software reliability engineering often relies on software reliability growth models (SRGMs) to identify and quantify defects and failures within a system.

Despite the availability of numerous SRGMs, assessing software reliability remains challenging due to the increasing complexity of modern software systems and their dynamic operational environments [179]. To address these challenges, researchers and practitioners in software engineering are exploring advanced approaches to improve reliability. Techniques such as predictive modeling, fault tolerance, deep learning, and machine learning are increasingly integrated with traditional SRGMs to enhance software dependability [180]. Predictive modeling, in particular, plays a vital role in software reliability engineering, as it enables early detection of potential issues during the development lifecycle, ensuring timely delivery and budget compliance.

Time series forecasting has proven especially useful for improving software reliability, as it uncovers underlying patterns and relationships in historical data, allowing for the development of more accurate and dependable reliability models [181]. Among the most widely used approaches in time series forecasting are ANN and ARIMA. ARIMA relies on historical time series data to predict future values based on observed trends and patterns, while ANN, inspired by the human brain, adapts to complex and nonlinear relationships within data [182].

ARIMA and SARIMA are widely used models for time series forecasting. ARIMA is primarily designed for non-seasonal data and consists of three components: Autoregressive, Integrated, and Moving Average. SARIMA, on the other hand, extends ARIMA by explicitly accounting for seasonal patterns in the data. It introduces additional parameters for seasonal auto-regression, seasonal differencing, and seasonal moving averages [183]. While ARIMA is suitable for datasets without seasonality, SARIMA is tailored to handle data with recurring seasonal fluctuations. In fact, ARIMA can be seen as a special case of SARIMA when no seasonal patterns are present, making SARIMA a more comprehensive framework for analyzing and forecasting time series data with seasonal behavior. In this study, a novel approach for software failure prediction is proposed by combining ANN and SARIMA with the Jaya optimization algorithm [184]. The hybrid model leverages ANN to capture nonlinear patterns and SARIMA to model linear and seasonal trends, resulting in enhanced forecasting performance compared to models that rely solely on one of these techniques. This approach addresses the challenges of SRP by integrating both linear and nonlinear patterns in software fault data. By optimizing the hybrid model using the Jaya algorithm, more accurate and reliable predictions are achieved [185]. The research investigates how the combination of ANN, SARIMA, and Jaya optimization can improve software fault prediction and reliability estimation. The underlying hypothesis is that this hybrid, Jaya-enhanced model will outperform traditional models in terms of predictive accuracy and adaptability to dynamic software environments.

5.2 Proposed Hybrid ANN-SARIMA using Jaya optimization Model

This study introduces a novel hybrid approach that merges SARIMA and ANN models with the Jaya optimization algorithm to improve time series forecasting accuracy in SRP. The process begins with the input reliability dataset, which undergoes data preparation involving cleaning, normalization, and partitioning into training and testing subsets to ensure consistency and reliability. The SARIMA component is first applied to capture linear trends, seasonal variations, and overall temporal patterns within the data. SARIMA effectively handles time dependent structures by combining autoregressive (AR), differencing (I), and moving average (MA) components, along with seasonal adjustments when required, producing an initial forecast that represents the linear behaviour of the data. While SARIMA efficiently models the linear aspects of the dataset, it fails to capture the nonlinear complexities often present in software reliability data. To address this limitation, residuals representing the differences between actual and SARIMA predicted values are computed, capturing the nonlinear and random variations unmodeled by SARIMA. These residuals are then passed to the ANN component, where a multilayer neural network with nonlinear activation functions such as ReLU or Tanh learns hidden patterns and nonlinear dependencies. Through back propagation, the ANN minimizes prediction errors and generates refined residual predictions. To further enhance model performance and ensure optimal configuration, the Jaya optimization algorithm is employed to automatically fine tune the parameters of ANN. Figure 5.1 illustrates the complete workflow of the proposed hybrid model, highlighting the seamless integration of SARIMA and ANN components to achieve robust software reliability forecasting.

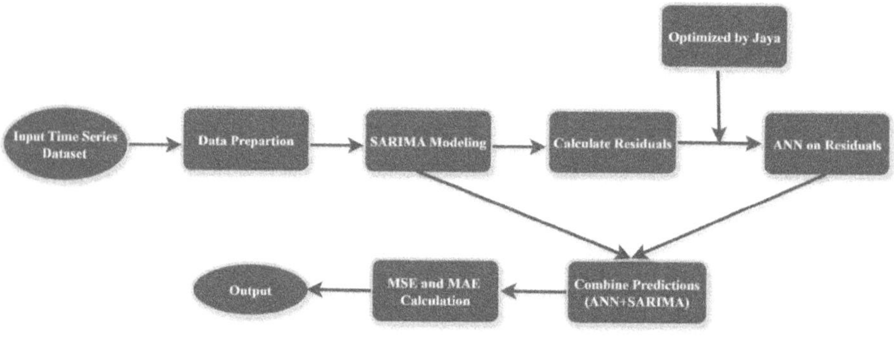

Fig. 5.1 Hybrid ANN-SARIMA flowchart utilizing the Jaya Model

The optimization process iteratively moves the solutions toward the best performing parameter combinations and away from the worst, using an objective function such as MSE or MAE until convergence is achieved. Once optimized, the ANN's predicted residuals are combined with the SARIMA forecasts, forming the final hybrid output that effectively integrates both linear and nonlinear components of the time series. The combined results are then evaluated using performance measures like MSE and MAE to assess the deviation between actual and predicted values. Experimental results confirm that this hybrid approach consistently outperforms traditional standalone models in terms of precision, robustness, and generalization. By uniting the strengths of SARIMA for modeling linear trends, ANN for capturing nonlinear patterns and Jaya for intelligent parameter optimization, the proposed hybrid framework delivers a powerful and adaptive forecasting mechanism. It effectively captures the dynamic and complex behavior of software reliability data, offering higher accuracy, lower forecasting errors, and greater efficiency. This integrated methodology demonstrates a balanced synergy between statistical modeling, neural computation, and metaheuristic optimization, resulting in a reliable and comprehensive predictive system suitable for complex real world software reliability forecasting tasks. Finally, the output from the ANN is combined with the SARIMA forecast, producing a comprehensive prediction that integrates both linear and nonlinear aspects of the time series.

$$\hat{y}_t^{(Hybrid)} = \hat{y}_t^{(SARIMA)} + r_t^{(ANN)} \tag{5.1}$$

Where $\hat{y}_t$ is the final forecast, $\hat{y}_t^{SARIMA}$ is the SARIMA forecast, and $\hat{y}_t^{ANN}$ is the ANN prediction of the nonlinear residuals.

5.2.1 Dataset

In this study, we assess the performance of our proposed model using three distinct fault detection datasets, following the methodology of [186]. Each dataset has unique characteristics and sources. Dataset DS-1 is derived from the JDT component of Eclipse version 2.0, containing 8,780 recorded faults over a span of 208 months. Dataset DS-2 comes from the platform component of Eclipse version 3.0, with 14,608 documented faults collected across 188 months. Dataset DS-3 is obtained from the networking component of the Linux operating system, including 2,251 faults recorded over a period of 193 months. These datasets provide essential benchmarks for testing the effectiveness and generalizability of our model across a range of fault detection scenarios.

5.2.2 Hyper-Parameters for ANN

The Hybrid ANN-SARIMA framework combines the strengths of ANN and SARIMA to enhance forecasting and prediction accuracy. The ANN is structured with three hidden layers containing 100, 50, and 25 neurons, each employing the hyperbolic tangent ("tanh") activation function. The "tanh" function is selected for its smoothness and continuity, which helps mitigate issues like vanishing gradients during training. It also enables the network to capture complex nonlinear relationships between inputs and outputs effectively. The model is compiled using the MSE loss function, providing a robust measure of prediction accuracy. Training is performed using the Adam optimizer, which efficiently adjusts the network weights based on gradient information. An early stopping mechanism is introduced to halt training if the validation loss does not improve for 50 consecutive epochs, thus preventing overfitting and unnecessary computation. To further enhance performance, the Jaya algorithm is employed as an intelligent optimizer, fine-tuning the ANN to model residuals from the SARIMA forecast more accurately. By focusing solely on performance-driven improvements, Jaya eliminates the need for manual hyperparameter tuning. It automatically determines the optimal number of hidden neurons, the most suitable activation function, and the appropriate learning rate for the ANN. This allows the network to capture nonlinear patterns in the residuals efficiently. Overall, the hybrid methodology bridges the linear modeling capability of SARIMA with the nonlinear learning power of ANN. As a result, it achieves enhanced predictive performance, improved accuracy, and significantly reduced error metrics. The combination of SARIMA and ANN, fine-tuned by Jaya optimization, ensures a more reliable and precise forecasting model suitable for complex time-series data.

Table 5.1 Experimental parameters of ANN-SARIMA hybrid model

Hyper-Parameter	Value/Description
Model Type	Artificial Neural Network (ANN)
Number of Hidden Layers	3
Neuron Count per Layer	Layer 1: 100
	Layer 2: 50
	Layer 3: 25
Activation function	Hyperbolic Tangent ("tanh")
Loss function	MSE
Optimizer	Adam
Learning Rate	Adaptive (based on Adam optimizer)
Batch Size	Variable (depending on implementation)
Epochs	Adaptive (with Early Stopping)
Data Train: Test Ratio	75:25

5.2.3 Performance Measures

Evaluating model accuracy often relies on well-known metrics such as MAE and MSE, which are calculated using Equations (5.2) and (5.3), respectively. MAE is defined as the average of the absolute differences between the observed values and the corresponding predicted values, and it provides a simple, non-negative measure of prediction accuracy. Lower MAE values indicate that the model's predictions are closer to the actual outcomes, thereby reflecting higher precision. Similarly, MSE is defined as the average of the squared differences between the observed and predicted values. By squaring the errors, MSE assigns greater weight to larger deviations, making it particularly sensitive to significant errors and outliers. Like MAE, MSE is always non-negative, and smaller MSE values correspond to better predictive performance. Together, these metrics offer complementary insights into model performance. MAE provides an intuitive interpretation of the average magnitude of prediction errors, while MSE emphasizes the impact of larger discrepancies. Using both metrics enables a more comprehensive evaluation of the model's reliability and robustness, ensuring that it captures general trends while effectively penalizing major prediction errors.

$$\boldsymbol{MAE} = \frac{\sum_{i=1}^{n} |yi-\hat{y}i|}{n} \tag{5.2}$$

$$\boldsymbol{MSE} = \frac{1}{n}\sum_{i=1}^{n}(yi-\hat{y}i)^2 \tag{5.3}$$

A hybrid SARIMA-ANN model aims to capture both linear and nonlinear patterns in the time series. The basic idea is to first apply the SARIMA model to capture the linear components and then use an ANN to model the residuals (nonlinear components).

$$\hat{y}_t^{(SARIMA)} = \emptyset_P\,(B)\Phi_P(B^s)(1-B)^d)(1-B^s)^D yt \tag{5.4}$$

$$r_t = y_t - \hat{y}_t^{(SARIMA)} \tag{5.5}$$

$$\hat{y}_t^{(ANN)} = \mathrm{f}\,(r_{t-1}\,,\ r_{t-2}\,,\ldots\ldots,r_{t-n}\ ;W) \tag{5.6}$$

$$\hat{y}_t^{(Hybrid)} = \hat{y}_t^{(SARIMA)} + r_t^{(ANN)} \tag{5.7}$$

$$\hat{y}_t = \emptyset_P\,(B)\Phi_P(B^s)(1-B)^d)(1-B^s)^D yt + \mathrm{f}\,(r_{t-1}\,,\ r_{t-2}\,,\ldots\ldots,r_{t-n}\ ;W) \tag{5.8}$$

Equation 5.4 represents the fit SARIMA model where $y_t$the observed time series at time t is, $\emptyset_P\,(B)$ and $\Phi_P(B^s)$ are polynomials of orders p and P for non-seasonal and seasonal auto regressive parts $(1-B)^d)$ *and* $(1-B^s)^D$ are the differencing terms for non-seasonal and seasonal parts respectively also B is the backshift operator. Eq. 5.5 and 5.6 used for calculate residuals and fit ANN model on residuals where f is a nonlinear function (often a multi-layer perceptron) and $r_{t-1}\,,\ r_{t-2}\,,\ldots\ldots,r_{t-n}$,are lagged observations , W represents the weights and biases of the neural network. Eq. 5.7 and 5.8 represents the forecast $\hat{y}_t$ as a combination of the SARIMA model's forecast and the ANN model's forecast on the residuals.

The Jaya optimization algorithm is a population-based optimization technique that iteratively improves solutions by considering the best and worst solutions in the population. To combine SARIMA and ANN using the Jaya optimization algorithm, you would define the objective function, which could be the MSE or MAE of the hybrid model. Next, you initialize the population by setting the SARIMA parameters and ANN weights. Finally, you use the Jaya algorithm to optimize these parameters and weights, aiming to minimize the objective function.

$$\hat{y}_t = \emptyset_P(B,\widehat{w})\Phi_P(B^s,\widehat{w})(1-B)^d)(1-B^s)^D yt + f(r_{t-1}, r_{t-2}, \ldots\ldots, r_{t-n}; \widehat{w}) \quad (5.9)$$

$\widehat{w}$ Is the optimized weight in Jaya optimization algorithm and Eq. 5.9 represents our hybrid model after optimization.

$$\text{MSE} = \frac{1}{n}\sum_{t=1}^{n}(y_t - \hat{y}_t^{(SARIMA)} - r_t^{(ANN)})^2 \quad (5.10)$$

$$\text{MAE} = \frac{1}{n}\sum_{t=1}^{n}|y_t - \hat{y}_t^{(SARIMA)} - r_t^{(ANN)}| \quad (5.11)$$

Eq. 5.10 and 5.11 are used for calculating the MSE and MAE of a hybrid ANN-SARIMA model. The MSE is a measure of the average squared difference between the actual values y_t and the predicted values $\hat{y}_t$ for a series of n observations. Eq. 5.10 measures the average squared error between the actual values and the values predicted by the hybrid model, thus giving a comprehensive measure of the model's performance. The MAE is a measure of the average absolute difference between the actual values y_t and the predicted values $\hat{y}_t$ for a series of n observations. Eq. 5.11 measures the average absolute error between the actual values and the values predicted by the hybrid model, providing a straightforward measure of the model's performance in terms of prediction accuracy.

5.2.4 Experiment Setup

The process commences with loading the dataset, followed by pre-processing steps to address any missing values or outliers. Subsequently, the dataset is divided into training and testing sets to facilitate further analysis. The Jaya Algorithm is then employed to automatically fine-tune the parameters of the ANN, including the delineation of the algorithm, formulation of the fitness function, and its execution. Following this, the SARIMA model undergoes training, with an optional step for fine-tuning its parameters. Concurrently, the ANN model is trained after standardizing the data and allows for adjustment of its hyperparameters as necessary. Next, both SARIMA and ANN models generate predictions, which are combined using averaging to produce a final forecast. The performance of the hybrid ANN-SARIMA model is evaluated using metrics such as MSE. The process concludes with the presentation of the evaluation results. Fig. 5.2 illustrates the execution of our proposed hybrid model.

To support our hypothesis, the following steps are taken:

Input: *Time series dataset of software failures*
Output: *Final prediction results with optimized ANN, MAE and MSE*
Steps:
Step 1. *Start*
Step 2. *Load Dataset*

- *Import the software failure dataset (e.g., cumulative failures over time).*

Step 3. *Preprocess Data*

- *Clean missing values, normalize if necessary.*
- *Ensure correct time formatting and indexing.*

Step 4. *Split Data*

- *Divide the dataset into training and testing subsets*

Step 5. *Model Training – SARIMA*

- *Select SARIMA(p, d, q)(P, D, Q)s parameters.*
- *Fit SARIMA model on the training set to capture linear patterns.*
- *Predict values using the SARIMA model:* $\hat{y}_t^{(SARIMA)}$
- *Calculate residuals:* $r(t) = y(t) - \hat{y}_t^{(SARIMA)}$

Step 6. *Model Training – ANN (Nonlinear Component)*

- *Use residuals (t)r(t) as inputs to the ANN model.*
- *Define ANN architecture (layers, neurons, activation functions).*
- *Initialize ANN parameters (weights, biases) randomly.*

Step 7. *Tuning ANN Parameters using Jaya Optimization)*

- *Objective: Minimize MAE and MSE from the hybrid model.*
- *initialize a population of ANN parameter vectors* $x_1 \in X$.

Evaluate fitness of each ANN using: $MSE = \frac{1}{n}\sum_{t=1}^{n}(r(t) - \hat{r}_{ANN}^{x_i}(t))^2$

Update population: $x_i^{new} = x_i + r_1(x_{best} - |x_i|) - r_2((x_{worst} - |x_i|)$

- *Select better solutions for the next generation.*
- *Repeat until convergence or max iterations.*
- *Return the best solution* x_{best} *as optimized ANN parameters.*

Step 8. *Hybrid Prediction Combination*

- *Use SARIMA to predict linear trends:* $\hat{y}_t^{(SARIMA)}$
- *Use optimized ANN to predict residuals:* $\hat{r}_t^{(ANN)}$

$$\hat{y}_t^{(Hybrid)} = \hat{y}_t^{(SARIMA)} + \hat{r}_t^{(ANN)}$$

Step 9. *Model Evaluation*

- *Compute final performance metrics:*
- $MAE = \frac{1}{n}\sum_{t=1}^{n}|y(t) - \hat{y}\,hybrid(t)|$
- $MSE = \frac{1}{n}\sum_{t=1}^{n}(y(t) - \hat{y}\,hybrid(t))^2$

Step 10. *Output Result*

- *Display and record final predictions, MAE, and MSE.*
- *Conclude reliability trend analysis.*

End

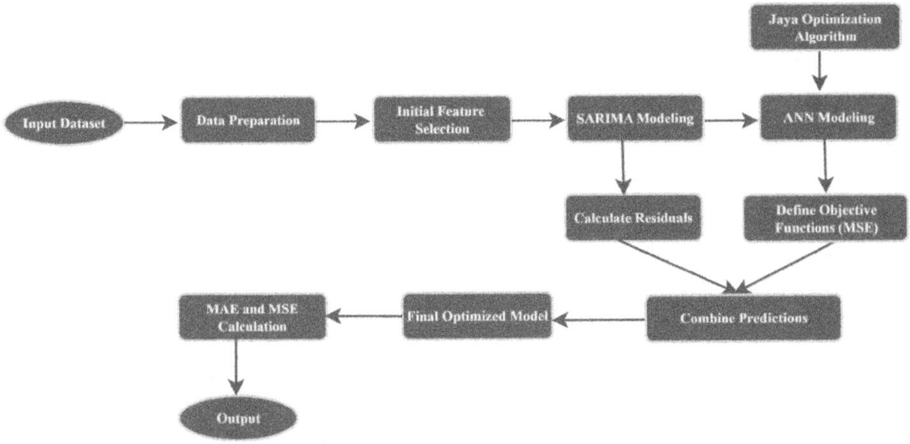

Fig. 5.2 Proposed hybrid ANN-SARIMA model

5.3 Result and Discussion

The empirical results of this study demonstrate that the hybrid ANN-SARIMA model consistently outperforms the individual SARIMA and ANN models across all datasets (DS1, DS2, and DS3), as evidenced by lower MSE and MAE values. A closer examination of the factors contributing to this improvement reveals the model's capacity to capture both linear and nonlinear patterns in software fault data. In DS1, where fault occurrences exhibit a linear decline, SARIMA effectively models the overall trend, while the ANN component captures minor nonlinear deviations caused by sporadic software changes, thereby enhancing overall predictive accuracy. In DS2, characterized by high fault density and clustered patterns from rapid development phases, SARIMA alone struggles with abrupt changes; however, ANN successfully manages these nonlinear clusters. Together, they form a robust solution that mitigates large errors and improves forecast precision. DS3, containing random and irregular fault patterns, presents challenges for both models individually, but the hybrid model balances weak linear trends and nonlinear randomness, resulting in more stable predictions and further reductions in MSE and MAE.

The superior performance of the hybrid model is also attributed to optimized parameter tuning of both SARIMA and ANN components using the Jaya algorithm. By calibrating SARIMA's autoregressive and moving average parameters alongside ANN's learning rate and neuron configuration, the hybrid model adapts to the unique characteristics of each dataset, preventing overfitting, particularly in DS3, where fault occurrences are highly irregular. This fine-tuning enhances the model's adaptability and predictive reliability. By combining SARIMA's strength in modeling long-term linear trends and seasonality with ANN's ability to capture short-term nonlinear fluctuations, the hybrid approach effectively addresses both types of fault patterns, consistently outperforming individual models. The Jaya algorithm ensures precise tuning for each dataset, contributing to lower prediction errors across all scenarios and demonstrating the hybrid model's robustness, flexibility, and superior effectiveness in improving SRPs.

Table 5.2 Result analysis and comparison of the ANN-SARIMA hybrid model on DS1

Model	DATASET	MSE	MAE
ARIMA	DS1	2.394	1.251
ANN		3.369	1.501
DSS		134169	345.49
FRE		123400	329.22
GO		135410.9	330.29
GGO		134468.3	339.74
ISS		135411.4	330.42
LGC		160680.9	377.92
TC		48205.2	181.62
Hybrid ANN -SARIMA		**2.421**	**0.55**

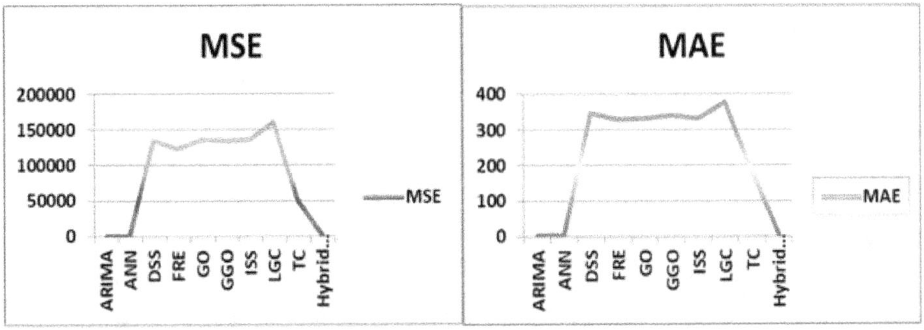

Fig. 5.3 Result comparison of the hybrid ANN-SARIMA model on DS1

Table 5.3 Result analysis and comparison of the ANN-SARIMA hybrid model on DS2

Model	DATASET	MSE	MAE
ARIMA	DS2	33.727	4.859
ANN		52.696	5.419
DSS		233692.8	388.77
FRE		220155.3	320.78
GO		389853.6	329.91
GGO		279821.9	404.80
ISS		300799.2	425.18
LGC		397974.9	528.42
TC		49445.7	141.51
Hybrid ANN -SARIMA		**7.029**	**2.979**

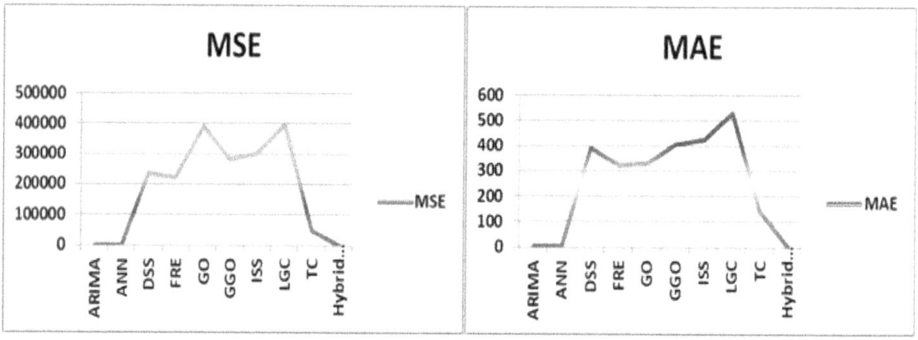

Fig. 5.4 Result comparison of the hybrid ANN-SARIMA model on DS2

Table 5.4 Result analysis and comparison of the ANN-SARIMA hybrid model on DS3

Model	DATASET	MSE	MAE
ARIMA	DS3	469.3	9.512
ANN		353.832	8.168
DSS		1139.5	26.547
FRE		3859.9	48.593
GO		14230.4	103.31
GGO		1096.1	25.608
ISS		1712.1	34.781
LGC		5109.2	60.994
TC		1231.1	26.232
Hybrid ANN -SARIMA		**308.162**	**2.873**

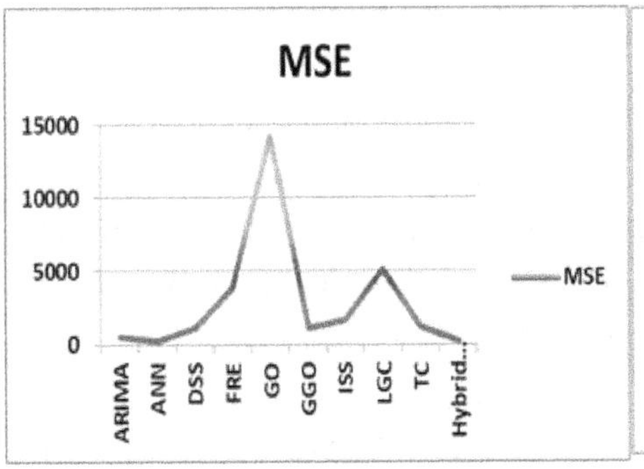

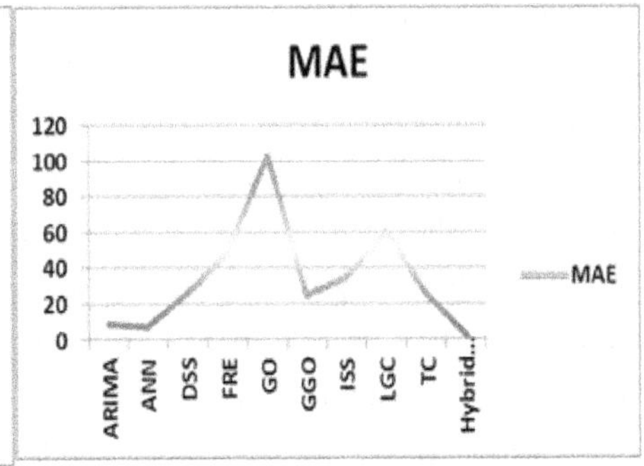

Fig. 5.5 Result comparison of the hybrid ANN-SARIMA model on DS3

We conducted an extensive analysis over 208 months for DS-1, during which 8,780 faults were recorded. Using the Akaike Information Criterion (AIC), SARIMA (1, 1, 0) was identified as the most suitable model for this dataset, which consisted of 158 training and 50 testing data points. Our evaluation revealed that the hybrid ANN-SARIMA model outperformed not only the individual ANN and ARIMA models but also seven other parametric models listed in Table 5.2.

Different models were evaluated on the DS1 dataset to measure their prediction accuracy using MSE and MAE values. The ARIMA model achieved an MSE of 2.394 and an MAE of 1.251, while the ANN model recorded slightly higher values with an MSE of 3.369 and an MAE of 1.501. The DSS model [187] produced very large errors with an MSE of 134,169 and an MAE of 345.49, and the FRE model [188,189] showed an MSE of 123,400 and an MAE of 329.22. Similarly, the GO model [190] reported an MSE of 135,410.9 and an MAE of 330.29, the GGO model [191] had an MSE of 134,468.3 and an MAE of 339.74, the ISS model [192] produced an MSE of 135,411.4 and an MAE of 330.42, the LGC model [193] showed an MSE of 160,680.9 and an MAE of 377.92, and the TC model [194] achieved an MSE of 48,205.2 and an MAE of 181.62. In comparison, the Hybrid ANN–SARIMA model demonstrated the best performance with an MSE of 2.421 and a very low MAE of 0.55, indicating its superior accuracy and reliability over all other models.

Moving on to DS-2, a 188-month dataset containing 14,608 errors, we allocated 138 points for training and 50 for testing. SARIMA (0, 1, 1) emerged as the best model according to the AIC criterion. Further analysis confirmed the hybrid ANN–SARIMA model's superiority, surpassing individual ANN and ARIMA models as well as other conventional SRGMs. Different models were tested on the DS2 dataset to evaluate their prediction performance using MSE and MAE values which is listed in Table 5.3 The ARIMA model achieved an MSE of 33.727 and an MAE of 4.859, while the ANN model showed slightly higher errors with an MSE of 52.696 and an MAE of 5.419. The DSS model produced an MSE of 233,692.8 and an MAE of 388.77, whereas the FRE model recorded an MSE of 220,155.3 and an MAE of 320.78. Similarly, the GO model had an MSE of 389,853.6 and an MAE of 329.91, the GGO model recorded an MSE of 279,821.9 and an MAE of 404.80, the ISS model showed an MSE of 300,799.2 and an MAE of 425.18, the LGC model achieved an MSE of 397,974.9 and an MAE of 528.42, and the TC model produced an MSE of 49,445.7 and an MAE of 141.51. In comparison, the Hybrid ANN–SARIMA model demonstrated the best results with an MSE of 7.029 and an MAE of 2.979, showing much higher prediction accuracy and reliability than all other models.

Finally, in DS-3, spanning 193 months with 2,251 recorded faults, we used 143 training and 50 testing points. SARIMA (1, 1, 0) was selected based on the AIC criterion, consistent with the methodology applied in DS-1. The hybrid ANN–SARIMA model again outperformed the standalone ANN and ARIMA models as well as other models listed in Table 5.5. Various models were evaluated on the DS3 dataset using MSE and MAE values to assess their predictive accuracy. The ARIMA model achieved an MSE of 469.3 and an MAE of 9.512, while the ANN model performed slightly better with an MSE of 353.832 and an MAE of 8.168. The DSS model recorded an MSE of 1,139.5 and an MAE of 26.547, whereas the FRE model produced an MSE of 3,859.9 and an MAE of 48.593. Similarly, the GO model showed an MSE of 14,230.4 and an MAE of 103.31, the GGO model had an MSE of 1,096.1 and an MAE of 25.608, the ISS model achieved an MSE of 1,712.1 and an MAE of 34.781, the LGC model recorded an MSE of 5,109.2 and an MAE of 60.994, and the TC model produced an MSE of 1,231.1 and an MAE of 26.232. In contrast, the Hybrid ANN–SARIMA model achieved the lowest errors with an MSE of 308.162 and an MAE of 2.873, demonstrating its superior prediction accuracy and robustness compared to all other models. A comprehensive comparison of the hybrid model's performance with other models is provided in Figures 5.3, 5.4, and 5.5 visually illustrate the results for DS-1, DS-2, and DS-3, respectively, highlighting the hybrid model's consistent superiority over existing approaches.

5.4 Chapter Summary and Future Scope

A major advancement in predicting accuracy within software reliability analysis is represented by Advancing Software Reliability forecasting with the Hybrid ANN-SARIMA Model. This model becomes a powerful fault prediction tool by combining the advantages of SARIMA and ANN. Through the integration of SARIMA's adept time series analysis capabilities and ANN's nonlinear learning capacity, the model attains remarkable accuracy in forecasting software faults. Performance Evaluation: Rigorous evaluation utilizing key metrics like MSE and MAE revealed the hybrid model consistently delivering low error rates across datasets (DS-1, DS-2, and DS-3), underscoring its precision. Benefits of Implementation: Implementation of the hybrid model in software reliability forecasting empowers decision-makers by enabling proactive identification and resolution of potential issues, ultimately enhancing decision-making processes. Moreover, by accurately predicting faults, the model contributes to minimizing system downtime, thereby elevating overall reliability and customer satisfaction.

5.4.1 Challenges

The hybrid SARIMA-ANN model enhanced by Jaya optimization has shown promising results in SRP but has room for improvement. Integrating additional data sources, such as code quality metrics and developer activity, could provide deeper insights into fault analysis. Future advancements could involve using machine learning paradigms like LSTM and CNN to capture complex fault patterns more effectively and employing reinforcement learning for real-time decision-making. Expanding the model's use to domains like cybersecurity, healthcare, and manufacturing could demonstrate its adaptability in anomaly detection and system failure prevention. Incorporating real-time prediction and online learning would allow continuous monitoring and dynamic adaptation, while optimizing computational efficiency through techniques like model pruning and parallel processing would make the model scalable for large, real-time applications.

CHAPTER:6 Conclusions and Future Scope

6.1 Thesis Summary

The reliability of software systems is a vital factor that directly influences their usability, performance, and overall success across diverse application domains. Predicting software reliability with accuracy continues to be a major challenge in software engineering because of the complex and dynamic behavior of fault occurrences. Conventional reliability prediction methods frequently lack precision, adaptability to evolving conditions, and computational efficiency. To address these challenges, this research integrates machine learning and statistical modeling approaches, specifically employing ANN, ELM, and SARIMA models. Furthermore, the study incorporates the Jaya optimization algorithm to fine-tune model parameters and enhance prediction accuracy. By combining these advanced methods, the proposed approach aims to deliver a more reliable, efficient and adaptive framework for SRP. The hybrid models proposed in the ML machine learning and statistical approaches, resulting in superior prediction capabilities. The research systematically evaluates these models on multiple datasets to validate their effectiveness in SRP.

The thesis begins with an exploration of traditional SRP models, outlining their advantages and shortcomings. Traditional models like ARIMA and linear regression exhibit limitations when applied to large-scale or complex datasets. To address these limitations, the research introduces a hybrid approach combining SARIMA with ANN, as well as an optimization-enhanced JAYA-ELM model. These hybrid techniques leverage the predictive strengths of NN along with the time-series forecasting capabilities of SARIMA, creating a more comprehensive approach to SRP. Through comprehensive experimental analysis, this study demonstrates that hybrid models consistently surpass standalone models in terms of accuracy, robustness, and computational efficiency. One of the key contributions of this research is the development and evaluation of the ANN-SARIMA and JAYA-ELM models. The ANN-SARIMA model integrates ANN's capability to learn complex nonlinear relationships with SARIMA's strength in capturing linear and seasonal dependencies, resulting in more accurate and stable reliability predictions. This fusion enables the model to effectively manage both short-term variations and long-term fault trends in software data, enhancing overall predictive accuracy and reliability estimation. In parallel, the JAYA-ELM model utilizes the Jaya optimization algorithm to enhance feature selection and improve accuracy while minimizing training duration. The study assesses the performance of these models using real-world datasets and benchmarks them against conventional statistical and machine learning approaches. Results indicate that the proposed hybrid models achieve notably higher accuracy and lower computational cost than traditional techniques.

The initial experiment evaluates the performance of the ELM model using the PC5 dataset from the Promise repository, which includes 17,000 samples and 40 features. In this experiment, the number of hidden neurons in the ELM is varied to examine its effect on both accuracy and training duration. The findings indicate that while a higher number of hidden neurons tends to enhance accuracy, it also results in longer computational time. for instance, when using 10 hidden neurons, the accuracy ranges between 0.967 and 0.977 with a training time of 0.0312 seconds, while increasing to 100 hidden neurons results in accuracies from 0.963 to 0.978 but with a training time of 0.3470 seconds. The JAYA-ELM hybrid model is then applied to the same dataset to optimize feature selection. The Jaya algorithm selects the most relevant features, significantly improving classification accuracy while reducing training time. The optimized model demonstrates better performance than standard ELM across all configurations. The JAYA-ELM model with 10 hidden neurons achieves accuracies between 0.963 and 0.977 in just 0.0310 seconds, demonstrating improved efficiency. The study is further extended to the Camel 1.4 dataset, containing 872 samples and 21 features. Consistent with previous observations, the JAYA-ELM model outperforms the standard ELM in both accuracy and training efficiency. These results confirm that the hybrid JAYA-ELM effectively reduces training time while sustaining high accuracy, demonstrating its practicality for SRP.

The second experiment investigates an ensemble learning approach that integrates multiple classifiers, including WSVMs, RF, and an APE model. The goal is to analyze whether an ensemble-based approach improves classification accuracy compared to individual classifiers. The experiment evaluates the models using the G-Mean measure, a metric that assesses the balance between sensitivity and specificity. Results indicate that the proposed APE model consistently outperforms Weighted-SVMs and RF classifiers. For instance, on the PC2 dataset, APE achieves an AUC of 0.92, significantly higher than Weighted-SVMs (0.54) and RF (0.74).

The enhanced version of APE, referred to as EAPE, further improves accuracy. When comparing classification results, EAPE achieves an accuracy of 0.94 on PC2, whereas Enhanced W-SVMs, Enhanced RF, and Enhanced ELM obtain 0.58, 0.76, and 0.81, respectively. These findings suggest that ensemble learning is an effective approach for improving classification accuracy in SRP. Additionally, the study explores the impact of feature selection on model performance. A forward Greedy Selection method is employed to refine feature selection, resulting in improved classification accuracy. The proposed ensemble model with feature selection achieves the highest G-Mean score, demonstrating its ability to handle imbalanced datasets effectively. The research confirms that ensemble learning, combined with feature selection, provides superior classification performance compared to traditional machine learning models.

The third experiment focuses on time-series forecasting for SRP using the hybrid ANN–SARIMA model. The study examines three datasets, DS-1, DS-2, and DS-3, covering software failure data over periods of 208, 188, and 193 months, respectively. The ANN–SARIMA hybrid model is evaluated using the MAE and MSE metrics. Results indicate that the hybrid model consistently outperforms the standalone models. In DS-2, the ANN–SARIMA model achieves an MSE of 2.421 and an MAE of 0.550, which are significantly lower than those of the ANN model, with an MSE of 3.369 and an MAE of 1.501, and the ARIMA model, with an MSE of 2.394 and an MAE of 1.251. Similar trends are observed in DS-1 and DS-3, confirming that the ANN–SARIMA model provides highly accurate and reliable forecasts for SRP.

This research establishes that hybrid models combining statistical and machine learning approaches significantly improve SRP. The JAYA-ELM model enhances feature selection and reduces computational time, making it highly efficient for classification tasks. Meanwhile, the ANN-SARIMA hybrid model demonstrates strong performance in time-series forecasting, outperforming traditional parametric models. The ensemble learning approach, particularly the Enhanced APE model, further boosts classification accuracy by integrating multiple classifiers.

6.2 Future Scope

Looking forward, multiple avenues can be pursued to further enhance SRP using machine learning approaches. One important approach involves integrating advanced optimization algorithms such as particle swarm optimization, genetic algorithms, and differential evolution to refine parameter tuning and improve predictive performance. These methods offer more adaptive exploration of the search space compared to traditional techniques, reducing overfitting and improving model generalization. Additionally, combining these optimization strategies with hybrid or ensemble learning frameworks could yield more robust and scalable reliability prediction models capable of handling complex software fault dynamics across diverse datasets. Real-time applications of these models in live software monitoring environments could provide valuable insights into their practical robustness and usability, enabling more proactive reliability management. Additionally, integrating explainability into machine learning models using approaches such as LIME (Local Interpretable Model-agnostic Explanations) or SHAP (SHapley Additive exPlanations) can enhance user trust and provide clearer insights into model predictions, particularly in critical software applications. Evaluating these models on larger and more diverse datasets across different software domains is another important step to verify their scalability and adaptability. Furthermore, multi-objective optimization frameworks could be investigated to balance trade-offs among accuracy, training time, and resource usage, which are key factors for practical, real-world deployment.

In addition, integrating deep learning models such as Long Short-Term Memory networks (LSTMs), Gated Recurrent Units (GRUs), or Convolutional Neural Networks (CNNs) with statistical methods can improve the modeling of long-term dependencies and complex patterns in software reliability data. Automated Machine Learning (AutoML) techniques can further streamline model design, hyperparameter tuning, and deployment, making these advanced predictive models more accessible to practitioners without specialized expertise.. Collaboration with software development teams is another critical area for future work. By bridging the gap between research and practice, predictive models can be effectively integrated into agile development processes or DevOps workflows, enabling real-time decision-making and reliability improvements. Such collaborations can also help identify practical challenges and refine the models for enhanced usability and impact. Finally, tackling challenges related to scalability, explainability, and real-time applicability will enable machine learning models to become essential tools in modern software engineering, significantly supporting the creation of reliable, robust, and efficient software systems. By leveraging these advancements and pursuing the identified future directions, the full potential of machine learning models for SRP can be unlocked, transforming the field and establishing new standards for software engineering practices.

www.ingramcontent.com/pod-product-compliance
Lightning Source LLC
LaVergne TN
LVHW021736071126
851857LV00040B/1448
9781962116626